U0039202

外國名人軼事一百則

100 ANECDOTES OF EMINENT PEOPLE

一百叢書 ㉜

英漢對照English-Chinese

王堅 華蘇揚 編譯

外國名人軼事一百則

100 ANECDOTES OF EMINENT PEOPLE

臺灣商務印書館發行

《一百叢書》總序

本館出版英漢（或漢英）對照《一百叢書》的目的，是希望憑藉着英、漢兩種語言的對譯，把中國和世界各類著名作品的精華部分介紹給中外讀者。

本叢書的涉及面很廣。題材包括了寓言、詩歌、散文、短篇小説、書信、演説、語錄、神話故事、聖經故事、成語故事、名著選段等等。

顧名思義，《一百叢書》中的每一種都由一百個單元組成。以一百為單位，主要是讓編譯者在浩瀚的名著的海洋中作挑選時有一個取捨的最低和最高限額。至於取捨的標準，則是見仁見智，各有心得。

由於各種書中被選用的篇章節段，都是以原文或已被認定的範本作藍本，而譯文又經專家學者們精雕細琢，千錘百煉，故本叢書除可作為各種題材的精選讀本外，也是研習英漢兩種語言對譯的理想參考書，部分更可用作朗誦教材。外國學者如要研習漢語，本書亦不失為理想工具。

商務印書館（香港）有限公司

編輯部

前言

世界名人的至言弘論、豐功偉業，相信無人不知。但他們的日常言行、生活瑣事，卻不一定廣泛流傳。他們這些一點一滴的生活經驗、思想感情往往都能反映他們的灼見及成就，甚至他們的歷史背景、社會時局。要瞭解他們，從他們的生活體驗中領略人生道理，就要閱讀關於他們的故事、傳記、自傳等。

閱讀傳記是一種文學鑑賞；從傳記裏可以欣賞到動人的描述，感受人情世故。閱讀名人軼事就有一種走近名人，與之對話的感覺。通過和他們的接觸，我們有如展開想像的翅膀，遨遊異國他鄉，和選篇中的人物同悲共樂。相信這會使我們生活豐富，更好地理解人生，實現人生理想。

《外國名人軼事一百則》涉及 11 個不同國家的名人 76 位，如哲學家蘇格拉底、伏爾泰、馬克思，科學家哥白尼、牛頓、達爾文、愛迪生、愛因斯坦，作家或詩人伊索、歌德、拜倫、巴爾扎克、狄更斯、馬克・吐溫、哈代，畫家達・芬奇、倫勃朗，音樂家貝多芬、瓦格納，政治家富蘭克林、林肯、列寧、邱吉爾、羅斯福等等。本書選篇中有些軼事已為人熟知，也有不少軼事是鮮為人知的。

本書的編譯有幾項標準。一，名人的軼事必須由知名人士講述，或由名人自述。二，選材中各界名人盡量兼顧。三，內容有趣，語言雋雅，敘述生動。四，考慮到學習語言的目的，漢譯文在保持通順的條件下，盡量貼近原文。

為讓讀者對選篇所涉及的名人有粗略的認識，特別提供名人簡介，各篇又附註釋若干，或註人物，或註語言，或介紹背景。為方便讀者查閱，全部一百篇軼事分為幾個大類，如哲學家、科學家、詩人、作家、畫家、音樂家、政治家等。各篇按名人出生年代先後順序排列。

本書的編譯工作進行艱辛。在茫茫書海中尋覓資料，精選名著版本，再要作出恰如其份的對照漢語譯文，絕非易事。幸虧賀善鏞先生在全書編譯過程中自始至終給予我們幫助，我們對此表示誠摯的謝意。我們還要特別感謝美國波特蘭州立大學洛伊絲·貝克教授為本書的編譯提供了可貴的參考書及意見。本書在編選和翻譯方面遠非盡善盡美，敬請讀者批評指教。

王 堅　華蘇揚

一九九九年五月

PREFACE

While the famous remarks and assertions and outstanding achievements and contributions of eminent people of the world may have been all too well known to most, their words and deeds in their daily lives may not have been so familiar. Such bits and pieces of their life experiences and thoughts and feelings nevertheless often reflect their brilliant views and achievements, and even their historical backgrounds and social environments. A reading of their stories, biographies or autobiographies will allow us to live through their experiences and understand them as much as the meanings of life.

Reading biographies is a kind of literary appreciation. From biographies we can appreciate exciting descriptions and experience touching emotions. Reading the anecdotes of famous people makes one feel one is approaching and communicating with the personages. By contacting them, we are like embarking on a journey on the wings of imagination to the exotic realms of their emotions. This will serve to enrich our life, help us understand it better and realize our life ideals as well.

100 Anecdotes of Eminent People involves 76 celebrities from 11 different countries — among others, philosophers like Socrates, Voltaire and Karl Marx; scientists like Copernicus, Newton, Darwin, Edison and Einstein; writers or poets like Aesop, Goethe, Byron, Balzac, Dickens, Mark Twain and Hardy; artists like da Vinci and Rembrandt; musicians like Beethoven and Wagner; and politicians like Franklin, Lincoln, Lenin, Churchill and F. Roosevelt. Some anecdotes in this book are quite familiar to the readers; but quite a number of the anecdotes may be fresh to them.

There are several criteria for the compilation and translation of the present collection. First, the anecdote of a celebrity to be worth reading must be told by a person or a biographer equally famous, or by the celebrity himself. Second, in the process of selection, we tried our best to choose the famous people representative of various fields. Third, the content has to be interesting, the language elegant, and the style lively. Finally, the Chinese translation is close to the English original without compromising fluency in Chinese, considering the purpose of language learning.

In order to provide readers with a general idea about the eminent people concerned, a brief introduction of the personage is given in each passage. Some notes are appended to it, either on the characters involved, or on the language, or on background information. To facilitate search, the 100 anecdotes are divided into several categories like Philosophers, Scientists, Poets, Writers, Artists, Musicians,

Politicians and so on. The passages are arranged in the chronological order of the years of birth of the celebrities.

The compilation of this book was carried out with toil and moil. It was by no means an easy task to seek for the best materials in a sea of books, select those best suited to the criteria mentioned above and come up with a translated version that is appropriate to the original. We are grateful to Mr. He Shanyong for his constant help at every stage of our work. Moreover, we would like to extend special thanks to Professor Lois Baker of Portland State University for providing us with invaluable reference books and her timely advice. Any comments and suggestions from the readers for improvement will be appreciated.

Wang Jian and Hua Suyang
May, 1999

Contents
目錄

Philosophers 哲學家

Scientists 科學家

Poets and Writers 詩人和作家

Artists and Musicians 藝術家與音樂家

Politicians 政治家

Others 其他

Philosophers
哲學家

1 Follow Me and Learn

Xenophon[1] was a man of great modesty, and as handsome as can be imagined. They say that Socrates met him in a narrow lane, and put his stick across it, and prevented him from passing by, asking where all kinds of necessary things were sold. And when Xenophon had answered him, he asked, again, where men were made good and virtuous. And as Xenophon did not know, Socrates said, "Follow me, then, and learn." And from that time forth Xenophon became a follower of Socrates.

— D. Laertius[2]

---

1. Xenophon (公元前約 431 — 355)：色諾芬，古希臘將領、歷史學家，Socrates 的學生，主要著作有《遠征記》(*Anabasis*)、《希臘史》(*Hellenica*)、《回憶蘇格拉底》(*Memorabilia*) 等。
2. Diogenes Laertius (公元 3 世紀)：累爾歐斯，希臘作家，著有《希臘哲學家生平》(*On the Lives of Greek Philosophers*).

一　學做人

色諾芬是個虛懷若谷的人，而且相貌堂堂，一表人才。據說，蘇格拉底在一條窄巷遇見他，把手杖橫在巷中，擋住他的去路，問他什麼地方有賣各種各樣的必需品。色諾芬答覆以後，蘇格拉底又問，什麼地方使人有教養、有道德。色諾芬不知道，蘇格拉底就說，“要是跟我學，就能學會。”於是從那時起，色諾芬就成了蘇格拉底的門徒。

——〔希臘〕累爾歇斯

名人簡介

Socrates（蘇格拉底）(公元前469—399)，古希臘哲學家，為西方文化的哲學思想奠基人之一，本人無著作傳世，他的學說見於他的學生色諾芬（Xenophon）和柏拉圖（Plato）的著作中。

2 Idleness Is Necessary

...he took life easily. He recommends idleness as necessary to the production of good mental work. He worked and meditated but a few hours a day: and most of those in bed. He used to think best in bed, he said. The afternoon he devoted to society and recreation. After supper he wrote letters to various persons, all plainly intended for publication, and scrupulously preserved. He kept himself free from care, and was most cautious about his health, regarding himself, no doubt, as a subject of experiment, and wishful to see how long he could prolong his life. At one time he writes to a friend that he shall be seriously disappointed if he does not manage to see 100 years.

— *O. J. Lodge*[1]

---

1. O. J. Lodge：Sir Oliver Joseph Lodge（洛奇）(1851—1940)，英國物理學家，提出太陽可能是無線電波源。著述甚多，如《電的現代觀》（*Modern Views of Electricity*, 1889）、《人和宇宙》（*Man and the Universe*, 1908）、自傳《流逝的歲月》（*Past Years*, 1931）等。

二　懶散

……他把生活看得很輕鬆。他建議說，要創造出腦力勞動的優秀成果，懶散些很有必要。他每天工作、思考只不過幾小時，而且大部分時間躺在牀上。他說他總是在牀上思考問題效果最好。他把下午的時間用在社交和娛樂活動上。晚飯後，他給各式各樣的人寫信。顯然，每封信都打算發表，便都慎重地保存起來。他從不讓自己煩惱，對自己的健康特別關注。毫無疑問，他把自己看作一個實驗對象，希望知道能把自己的壽命延長多久。一次，他在給一位朋友的信中說，要是活不到一百歲，他會十分失望。

——〔英〕洛奇

名人簡介

René Descartes（笛卡爾）(1596—1650)，法國哲學家、自然科學家、解析幾何學的奠基人，主要著作有《方法談》(*Discours de la methodé*, 1637)、《哲學原理》(*Principia philosophiae*, 1644)等。

3 A Cruel Hardship

At the age of fifty-three he[1] was sent for to Stockholm by Christina, Queen of Sweden, a young lady enthusiastically devoted to study of all kinds and determined to surround her Court with all that was most famous in literature and science. Thither, after hesitation, Descartes went. He greatly liked royalty, but he dreaded the cold climate. Born in Touraine, a Swedish winter was peculiarly trying to him, especially as the energetic Queen would have lessons given her at five o'clock in the morning. She intended to treat him well, and was immensely taken with him; but this getting up at five o'clock on a November morning, to a man accustomed all his life to lie in bed till eleven, was a cruel hardship.

— *O. J. Lodge*[2]

---

1. he：指René Descartes（笛卡爾）。本篇軼事提供了他在瑞典斯德哥爾摩去世的背景。
2. O. J. Lodge：洛奇，詳見第 2 篇的註釋。

三　苦不堪言

他五十三歲那年，被瑞典女王克里斯蒂娜請到斯德哥爾摩。女王還很年輕，熱衷於學習各種知識，並決意把宮廷沉浸在文學和科學的精華裏。笛卡爾經過猶豫也就去了。他很喜歡皇族，可是寒冷的氣候讓他望而生畏。對於出生在法國都蘭地區的笛卡爾來說，瑞典的冬季就特別難捱，尤其是精力充沛的女王要求在清晨五點鐘便開始上課。女王有意善待他，而且非常器重他。可是，十一月裏清早五點就起牀的做法，對一個一生都習慣於躺到上午十一點的人來說，卻是苦不堪言。

——〔英〕洛奇

名人簡介

René Descartes（笛卡爾）（1596-1650）：詳見第 2 篇。

4 Sitting in the Bastille

The twenty-one-year-old littérateur[1] is sitting in a cafe storming and raging against King and Court, and in particular deriding the dissolute Orleans[2]. His auditor, an officer whom he has met by accident, imperceptibly draws him out more and more. The young political poet begins to exaggerate and in an excess of zeal he boasts of having composed certain French and Latin lampoons which were being circulated anonymously at that time and had in reality been written by someone else. The spy promptly reported all this, the Regent learned of it, and a few days later Voltaire is sitting in the Bastille[3], where he has brought from his parents' house two

---

1. ...littérateur：指 Voltaire (伏爾泰)。
2. Orleans：奧爾良公爵。五歲的路易十五繼王位後，法國進入攝政時期，奧爾良為攝政王。
3. the Bastille：14 至 18 世紀法國的巴黎城堡和國家監獄。

四　坐牢

這位年方二十一的文人當時正坐在咖啡店裏對國王和朝廷極盡斥責攻擊之能事。其間，還特別把生活放蕩的奧爾良公爵嘲弄了一番。聽者是一位他偶然遇到的軍官，引他不知不覺地愈說愈多。年輕的政治詩人乘着興致開始夸夸其談。他誇口說，時下正在流傳某些匿名的法文和拉丁文的諷刺文章就是他的手筆。當然，這些作品實際上都是別人寫的。這個密探立即向上司報告了一切。攝政王也知道了這情況。幾天之後，伏爾泰便坐在巴士底獄的牢房裏。在那兒，他從父母家裏帶來了兩冊荷馬的書、兩塊繡

名人簡介

Voltaire（伏爾泰）(1694—1778)，法國啟蒙思想家、作家、哲學家，兩次被捕入獄，曾被逐出國，著有《哲學書簡》(*Lettres philosophiques*, 1734)、悲劇《扎伊爾》(Zaire, 1732)、小說《老實人》(*Candide*, 1759)、歷史著作《路易十四世的年代》(*Le Siècle de Louis XIV*, 1751)等。

volumes of Homer, two lace handkerchiefs, a hood, two collars, a night-cap, and a bottle of carnation perfume.

He sits in the tower for eleven months; and since he is not allowed to have paper and ink, he writes his verses with a piece of lead, between the lines of a book.

— E. Ludwig[4]

---

4. Emil Ludwig (1881—1948)：路德維格，德國作家，除劇本、詩歌、散文外，著有名人傳記多部，如《歌德傳》(*Goethe*, 1920)、《拿破侖傳》(*Napoleon*, 1925)、《林肯傳》(*Lincoln*, 1929)、《貝多芬傳》(*Beethoven*, 1943)等。

花邊手帕、一頂風帽、兩個領圈、一頂睡帽，外加一瓶石竹香水。

他在巴士底獄塔樓裏坐了十一個月的牢。由於獄方不讓他有紙張和墨水，他只好用鉛塊把自己的詩文寫在一本帶來的書的行間空白處。

——〔德〕路德維格

5 His Intimate

Voltaire[1], towards the close of his thirties, has returned, and after a period of hiding he now makes no further attempt to conceal his presence. He moves about from place to place, and finally locates with this grain-dealer, whom he also gets to act as his broker in grain speculations. In his quarters here Voltaire receives every one. Today the Duchess of Saint-Pierre and her friend are visiting him; and they have brought with them a woman who, though not exactly beautiful, is very striking in appearance. ... She enters unpretentiously — yet she is highly educated and has had a world of experience. ... From this evening on, she remained his intimate for seventeen years, first as his mistress and later as friend and patroness. For whole years he lives in the family chateau on the border of Lorraine[2] so as to be able, during his periodic persecutions, to get out of the country at a moment's notice.

— *E. Ludwig*[3]

---

1. Voltaire（伏爾泰）：他於1726—28 年流亡英國。本篇描寫他回法國後遇見夏德萊夫人(Mme du Châtelet)。她不滿與夏德萊侯爵的婚姻，卻與伏爾泰志同道合，在當時的文學界傳為佳話。
2. Lorraine： 洛林，當時不屬法國管轄，夏德萊夫人協助伏爾泰躲避迫害，他倆隱居在那裏的一座城堡裏。伏爾泰得以專心寫作。
3. E. Ludwig ：路德維格，詳見第 4 篇的註釋。

五　知己

伏爾泰快四十歲的時候回來了，經歷了一些躲躲藏藏的日子後，他現在決定不再躲藏。他到處走動，最後在糧商那裏住下來。這位糧商也是他做糧食生意的經紀人。伏爾泰在這兒的住所會見一切來客。今天，聖皮埃爾公爵夫人和她的朋友來拜訪他。這回隨她們同來的還有一位不算漂亮，但外貌卻很動人的女士。……她毫不做作地走了進來。她受過極好的教育，而且經驗豐富。……從那晚起，她成了伏爾泰的知己，起初是他的情人，後來是朋友和資助人。這種關係保持了十七年之久。這些年間，伏爾泰一直住在洛林邊界處的私家城堡裏。這樣，在他遇到間歇的迫害時，就可以隨時逃離法國。

——〔德〕路德維格

名人簡介

Voltaire（伏爾泰）（1694-1778）：詳見第 4 篇。

6 The First Volume Was Burnt

How well I still remember that night, when Mill[1] came to tell us, pale as Hector's[2] ghost, that my unfortunate first volume was burnt.

...

Mill had borrowed that first volume of my poor *French Revolution*... Well, one night about three weeks ago, we sat at tea, and Mill's short rap was heard at the door: Jane[3] rose to welcome him; but he stood there unresponsive, pale, the very picture of despair; ... After some considerable additional gasping, I learned from Mill this fact: that my poor manuscript, all except some four tattered leaves, was annihilated! He had left it out (too carelessly); it had been

---

1. Mill（穆勒）：他曾為Carlyle寫作《法國革命》提供參考書、出主意。但當他把 Carlyle 的手稿借回家細讀的過程中，手稿被女傭燒燬。
2. Hector：赫克托耳，荷馬作的古希臘史詩《伊利亞特》（*Iliad*）中的英雄，特洛伊戰爭中特洛伊的主將。他作戰勇猛，最後被希臘聯軍的阿喀琉斯擊斃。
3. Jane：本文作者卡萊爾的夫人。

六　書稿燒燬

我還很清楚記得那個晚上。穆勒臉色蒼白，就像赫克托耳的亡魂，跑來告訴我們，我那倒霉的第一卷書稿燒掉了。

……

穆勒借走了拙著《法國革命》第一卷，…… 嗯，大約三週前的一個晚上，我們正坐着喝茶，聽到穆勒短促的敲門聲。珍妮站起身去迎他，可他只是站在那兒毫無反應，面色蒼白，一副絕望的模樣。……他又氣喘了好一陣之後，我才從他説話中弄清了一個事實：我那可憐的手稿，除了破損的四頁之外，全部都燬了！他沒考慮到這點（太粗心大

名人簡介

John Stuart Mill（穆勒）(1806—1873)，英國哲學家、經濟學家和邏輯學家。他父親 James Mill 是哲學家、歷史學家和經濟學家，是功利主義哲學的主要代表。按照他父親的要求，從三歲起就接受系統的教育，十四歲訪問法國，對法國的文學、政治和社會深感興趣。主要著作有《邏輯體系》(*System of Logic*, 1843)、《政治經濟學原理》(*Principles of Political Economy*, 1848)、《論自由》(*On Liberty*, 1859)等。

taken for waste paper. ... Mill, whom I had to comfort and speak peace to, remained injudiciously enough till almost midnight, ...

— *T. Carlyle*[4]

---

4. Thomas Carlyle (1795 — 1881)：卡萊爾，英國散文作家和歷史學家，所著《法國革命》為他贏得了聲譽。此處所選第一小段是他多年後對書稿燒燬一事的回憶；第二大段是節選自他書燬不久後給他弟弟信中描述的事情經過。

意了）；別人把書稿當成了廢紙。……我不得不安慰穆勒，不說責怪的話。可他始終是精神恍惚，幾乎延續到半夜。

——〔英〕卡萊爾

7 A Man of Science

Science was for Marx a historically dynamic, revolutionary force. However great the joy with which he welcomed a new discovery in some theoretical science whose practical application perhaps it was as yet quite impossible to envisage, he experienced quite another kind of joy when the discovery involved immediate revolutionary changes in industry, and in historical development in general. For example, he followed closely the development of the discoveries made in the field of electricity and recently those of Marcel Deprez[1].

— *Friedrich Engels*[2]

---

1. Marcel Deprez (1843—1918)：馬賽爾．德普勒，法國工程師，電力輸送實驗的先驅。
2. Friedrich Engels (1820—1895)：恩格斯，德國社會主義哲學家，科學共產主義奠基人之一、國際無產階級的領袖，馬克思的朋友和戰友，與馬克斯合著《共產黨宣言》，整理和出版了《資本論》第2、3卷，重要著作還有《家庭、私有制和國家的起源》(*The Origin of the Family, Private Property and the State*, 1884)等。

七　科學巨人

在馬克思看來，科學是一種在歷史上充滿勃勃生機的革命力量。他對某門理論科學的一項新發現，總是抱歡迎的態度，心情無比喜悦。儘管對這一發現的實際應用，也許還未能預見，雖然如此，當這個發現能立即給工業、給歷史總體發展帶來革命性變化的時候，他就感到另一種截然不同的欣喜。例如，他曾密切地關注過電學領域中諸多發現的進展情況，最近還關注了馬賽爾·德普勒的一些發現。

——〔德〕恩格斯

名人簡介

Karl Marx（馬克思）(1818—1883)，生於德國，馬克思主義的創始人、科學共產主義的奠基人、國際無產階級的領袖，重要著作有《共產黨宣言》(*The Communist Manifesto*, 1848, 與恩格斯合寫)、《資本論》(*Das Kapital*, 1867) 等。

Scientists 科學家

8 Living to See It Appear

This famous work, *De Revolutionibus Orbium Coelestium*, embodied all his[1] painstaking calculations, applied his new system to each of the bodies in the solar system in succession, and treated besides of much other recondite matter. Towards the close of his life it was put into type. He can scarcely be said to have lived to see it appear, for he was stricken with paralysis before its completion; but a printed copy was brought to his bedside and put into his hands, so that he might just feel it before he died.

— *O. J. Lodge*[2]

1. his：指 Nicolaus Copernicus（哥白尼）。
2. O. J. Lodge：洛奇，詳見第 2 篇的註釋。

八　不朽的遺產

《天體運行論》這部名著包含了哥白尼費盡苦心的全部計算工作。在該書中，他把新運行體制一個一個地運用到太陽系的天體中。除此之外，該書還探討了其他不少鮮為人知的內容。在這位科學家即將離開人世的時候，他的大作交付排版。由於哥白尼在書稿排版完成之前患病癱瘓，幾乎可以說, 他未能在有生之年看到自己的著作問世。不過一本已經印好的書送到了哥白尼的牀邊，放到他手裏，好讓他在臨終前可以觸摸一下這本書。

——〔英〕洛奇

名人簡介

Nicolaus Copernicus（哥白尼）(1473—1543)，波蘭天文學家，創立太陽是宇宙的中心的日心説，否定了在西方統治了一千多年的地心説。這是天文學上一次偉大的革命，引起了人類宇宙觀的重大革新，使自然科學開始從神學中解放出來，著有《天體運行論》(*De Revolutionibis Orbium Coelestium*, 1543)。

9 An Artificial Nose

A quarrel at some feast, on a mathematical point, with a countryman led to the fixing of a duel, and it was fought with swords at 7 p.m. at the end of December, ... The result of this insane performance was that Tycho got his nose cut clean off.

He managed however to construct an artificial one, some say of gold and silver, some say of putty and brass; but whatever it was made of there is no doubt that he wore it for the rest of his life, and it is a most famous feature. It excited generally far more interest than his astronomical researches. It is said, moreover, to have very fairly resembled the original, but whether this remark was made by a friend or by an enemy I cannot say. One account says that he used to carry about with him a box of cement to apply whenever his nose came off, which it periodically did.

— O. J. Lodge[1]

---

1. O. J. Lodge：洛奇，詳見第 2 篇的註釋。

九　假鼻

在一次宴會上，布拉赫就數學問題與一個同胞的爭執引起了一場決鬥。決鬥以鬥劍方式定於十二月末的一個晚上七點鐘進行。這一愚蠢行為的後果是，布拉赫的鼻子給人整個切了下來。

不過他想法做了個假鼻子。有人說鼻子是用金和銀做的。也有人說是用油灰和黃銅做的。不論假鼻子是什麼材料做的，有一點毫無疑問，就是他從此一生都戴着這個假鼻子。這是個人人皆知的特徵。通常這個特徵遠比他的天文學研究工作更能激起人們的興趣。此外，據說這個替代品和真鼻子極為相似。不過這話是出自朋友之口，還是仇敵所說，我可就說不準了。有一篇報導還稱，布拉赫總是隨身帶着一盒黏固粉，用以修補時而掉落的鼻子。

——〔英〕洛奇

名人簡介

Tycho Brahe（第谷．布拉赫）(1546—1601)，丹麥天文學家，他大量觀測的資料為開普勒（Kepler）行星運動三定律奠定了基礎。

10 The Determining Influence

Tycho's uncle gave him what he would never have got at home — a good education and ultimately put him to study law. At the age of thirteen he entered the University of Copenhagen, and while there occurred the determining influence of his life. ...

Well, the boy Tycho, among others, watched for this eclipse on August 21st, 1560; and when it appeared at its appointed time, every instinct for the marvellous, dormant in his strong nature, awoke to strenuous life, and he determined to understand for himself a science permitting such wonderful possibilities of prediction. He was sent to Leipzig with a tutor to go on with his study of law, but he seems to have done as little law as possible: he spent all his money on books and instruments, and sat up half the night studying and watching the stars.

— *O. J. Lodge*[1]

1. O. J. Lodge：洛奇，詳見第 2 篇的註釋。

十　決定性的影響

布拉赫的叔父讓他接受了良好的教育。這是他呆在家裏永遠都不可能得到的。最後，叔父讓他去學法律。他十三歲那年進入哥本哈根大學學習。也正是在那裏產生了對他一生有決定性的影響。……

這個叫布拉赫的男孩，和其他人一起，觀看了發生在1560年8月21日的一次日蝕。當日蝕在預定的時間發生的時候，蟄伏在他堅強個性中全部非凡的本能，迎着奮發有為的人生復甦了。他決心要獨自地通曉一門讓他能如此奇妙地預測的科學。他在一名學監陪同下到來比錫繼續學習法律。不過他的法律好像學得盡可能的少。他把所有的錢都花在購買書籍和儀器上。晚上則熬到半夜，研究和觀察星體。

——〔英〕洛奇

名人簡介

Tycho Brahe (第谷．布拉赫)(1546－1601)：詳見第9篇。

11 A Meeting of Two Great Men

...and so he was to be kept isolated.

And then there came one more crushing blow. His eyes became inflamed and painful — the sight of one of them failed, the other soon went; he became totally blind. ...

He was now allowed an amanuensis, ...visitors also were permitted, ...many visited him, among them a man as immortal as himself — John Milton[1], then only twenty-nine, travelling in Italy. Surely a pathetic incident, this meeting of these two great men — the one already blind, the other destined to become so. No wonder that, as in his old age he dictated his masterpiece the thoughts of the English poet should run on the blind sage of Tuscany[2], and the reminiscence of their conversation should lend colour to the poem.

— *O. J. Lodge*[3]

---

1. John Milton (1608 — 1674)：彌爾頓，英國詩人。1638 — 39 年他曾到法國和意大利旅遊。 1652年他因勞累過度而雙目失明。主要作品有長詩《失樂園》(*Paradise Lost*, 1667)、《復樂園》(*Paradise Regained*, 1671)等。
2. Tuscany：意大利地區名，伽利略的出生地 Pisa 以及度過晚年的 Florence 都屬該地區。
3. O. J. Lodge：洛奇，詳見第 2 篇的註釋。

十一　偉人相聚

……就這樣不讓他與人來往。

此後，又有一次更具毀滅性的打擊。他的雙目開始紅腫疼痛——先是一隻眼睛的視力喪失，不久，另一隻的視力也喪失了。他完全失明了。……

他失明後，允許他有一名聽寫員，……還允許人來探望。來訪者很多，其中有一位和他同樣是不朽的人物——約翰．彌爾頓；那時才二十九歲，正在意大利旅遊。無疑，兩位偉人這次的會面是件令人生憐的事——一位已經雙目失明，而另一位也注定要失明。難怪，這位英國詩人晚年讓人筆錄他的傑作時，時常會想起托斯卡納的那位雙目失明的賢哲，他對兩人談話的回憶也會為他的詩作增色不少吧。

——〔英〕洛奇

名人簡介

Galileo Galilei（伽利略）(1564—1642)，意大利物理學家、天文學家。他推翻了奉為權威的亞里士多德關於“物體落下的速度和重量成比例”的學說。他支持和發展哥白尼的地動說。1633 年他遭到羅馬教廷的判罪管制。

12 A Great Publication

In 1601, Kepler was appointed "Imperial mathematician," to assist Tycho[1] in his calculations. ... and the tables upon which Tycho was now engaged are well called the Rudolphine[2] tables.

These tables of planetary motion Tycho had always regarded as the main work of his life; but he died before they were finished, and on his death-bed he intrusted the completion of them to Kepler, who loyally undertook their charge. ...

Still he worked on at the Rudolphine tables of Tycho, and ultimately, with some small help from Vienna[3], completed them; but he could not get the means to print them. He applied to the Court till he was sick of applying: they lay

---

1. Tycho：指 Tycho Brahe (第谷．布拉赫)，詳見第 9 篇。
2. Rudolphine：人名 Rudolf 的形容詞。Rudolf I (1218—1291)，魯道夫一世，神聖羅馬帝國皇帝，奪取了奧地利歸入自己的王朝。Rudolf II (1552—1612)，魯道夫二世，神聖羅馬帝國皇帝，奧地利大公。
3. Vienna：維也納，為奧地利首都，當時奧地利帝國在德意志諸邦中佔最重要的地位。

十二　一部大作

1601年，開普勒被任命為皇室數學家，協助布拉赫的計算工作。……布拉赫那時編製的圖表，現在人們因而稱之為魯道夫表。

布拉赫始終把編製這些行星運行表視為終生的重要工作。但是他沒完成行星表便去世了。他臨終前，把完成編製行星表的任務託付給了開普勒。開普勒便忠實地承擔了這項職責。……

此後他繼續編製布拉赫的魯道夫表。最終，在維也納方面提供的微薄資助下，圖表編製完成。可是開普勒卻籌集不到排印這些圖表的經費。他不斷向宮廷提出申請，直

名人簡介

Johannes Kepler（開普勒）(1571—1630)，德國天文學家，發現行星運動三大定律，探討大氣折射問題，為牛頓發現萬有引力定律和近代光學奠定了基礎。

idle four years. At last he determined to pay for the type himself. What he paid it with, God knows, but he did pay it, and he did bring out the tables, and so was faithful to the behest of his friend.

This great publication marks an era in astronomy.

— *O. J. Lodge*[4]

4. O. J. Lodge：洛奇，詳見第 2 篇的註釋。

至對申請感到膩煩。就這樣，圖表被閒置了四年。最後，開普勒決定自己支付排印的費用。他用什麼辦法支付，只有天知道。不過他確實付了錢，也確實使這些圖表得以問世。就這樣，他對朋友的囑託盡職守信。

這部大作標誌着天文學上的新紀元。

——〔英〕洛奇

13 Wait a Century

The astronomer Kepler, whose work on the planetary motions is now a classic, is reported to have said of his book that "it may wait a century for a reader, as God has waited 6000 years for an observer."

— *M. J. Adler*[1]

1. Mortimer Jerome Adler (1902—)：阿德勒，美國哲學家和教育家，《大英百科全書》董事會主席。

十三　等待一百年

天文學家開普勒有關行星運行的著作現今已是一部經典之作。據說他曾這樣說過自己的書："也許這本書要等上一百年才會有一個讀者，就像上帝等了六千年才等到了一個天文觀察者一樣。"

——〔美〕阿德勒

名人簡介

Johann Kepler（開普勒）(1571－1630)，詳見第 12 篇。

14 Endless Time Is Needed

...all Europe knew about him. Peter the Great[1] of Russia came to pay his respects to him, and the Queen of England journeyed to Delft[2] only to look at the wonders to be seen through the lenses of his microscopes. He exploded countless superstitions for the Royal Society[3], and aside from Isaac Newton and Robert Boyle[4] he was the most famous of their members. ...

...

"The professors and students of the University of Leyden[5] were long ago dazzled by my discoveries, they hired three lens-grinders to come to teach the students, but what came of it?" wrote that independent Dutchman.

"Nothing, so far as I can judge, for almost all of the

---

1. Peter the Great (1672—1725)：彼得大帝，俄國沙皇，曾於1697—98年周遊歐洲幾個國家。
2. Delft：代爾夫，荷蘭城市，列文虎克出生和長期生活在這裏。
3. the Royal Society：(英國)皇家學會。
4. Robert Boyle (1627—1691)：玻意耳，英國物理學家、化學家和自然哲學家，倫敦皇家學會創始人之一，確立了在恆溫下氣體體積與壓力成反比的"玻意耳定律"。
5. Leyden：萊頓，荷蘭城市名。

十四　鞠躬盡瘁

……他享譽整個歐洲。俄國彼得大帝來看望過他，英國女王專程來過代爾夫，唯一的目的就是看看他顯微鏡透鏡下的奇蹟。他為皇家學會破除了無數的迷信，除牛頓和玻意耳兩人外，他是學會會員中最有名的。……

……

這個個性獨立的荷蘭人寫道：

“萊頓大學的師生早就被我的發現弄得眼花繚亂。他們聘請了三個磨鏡片工人來教學生。可是有什麼結果呢？”

“我想，什麼結果也沒有，因為他們在學校教的課程幾

名人簡介

Antony van Leeuwenhoek（列文虎克）(1632—1723)，荷蘭生物學家、顯微鏡學家，最先用自製的透鏡觀察細菌和原生動物，發現精子、血紅細胞和水中微生物。

courses they teach there are for the purpose of getting money through knowledge or for gaining the respect of the world by showing people how learned you are, and these things have nothing to do with discovering the things that are buried from our eyes. I am convinced that of a thousand people not one is capable of carrying out such studies, because endless time is needed and much money is spilled and because a man has always to be busy with his thoughts if anything is to be accomplished...."

... In 1723, when he was ninety-one years old and on his deathbed, he sent for his friend Hoogvliet.... He mumbled:

"Hoogvliet, my friend, be so good as to have those two letters[6] on the table translated into Latin.... Send them to London to the Royal Society...."

— *P. de Kruif*[7]

---

6. two letters：列文虎克把自己的研究工作情況隨時向英國皇家學會報告。他與學會保持聯繫，直到逝世，歷時五十餘年。
7. Paul de Kruif (1890—1971)：德克賴夫，美國細菌學家和作家，主要著作有《細菌獵索者》(*Microbe Hunters*, 1926)、《為生命而搏鬥》(*The Fight for Life*, 1939)、《健康就是財富》(*Health Is Wealth*, 1940)等。

乎都是為了利用知識賺錢，或者向人們顯示他們多麼有學問，以此得到全世界的尊敬。這些事情都與發現我們肉眼看不見的東西無關。我相信一千個人當中沒有一個人能夠進行這種研究，因為這需要無限的時間，要白花很多錢，還因為你得整天不停地思考，才會做成一點事情。……”

……1723年他91歲，躺在病榻上，臨死之前，讓人找來他的朋友胡列特。……他口齒不清地說：

“胡列特，老兄，麻煩你把桌上的兩封信譯成拉丁文。……寄到倫敦皇家學會去。……”

——〔美〕德克賴夫

15 Extreme Absence

Anecdote of Newton, showing his extreme absence; inviting a friend to dinner and forgetting it: the friend arriving, and finding the philosopher in a fit of[1] abstraction. Dinner brought up for one; the friend (without disturbing Newton) sitting down and dispatching it, and Newton, after recovering from his reverie, looking at the empty dishes and saying[2], "Well really, if it wasn't for the proof before my eyes, I could have sworn that I had not yet dined."

— *T. Moore*[3]

---

1. a fit of：(某種感情等的)突發。
2. ... saying：以上各句在語法結構上不完整，動詞均用了分詞形式。原文是日記，故行文類似寫提綱、計劃、筆記等，盡可能簡略。
3. Thomas Moore (1779—1852)：穆爾，英國詩人、作家、音樂家，詩人拜倫和雪萊的朋友，主要作品有《愛爾蘭歌曲集》(*Irish Melodies*, 1807)、敘事詩《拉拉．魯克》(*Lalla Rookh*, 1817)等。

十五　心不在焉

表明牛頓極度心不在焉有以下的軼事。請了朋友來吃飯，卻把這件事忘掉了。朋友來了，發覺這位大哲人正在出神凝思。端上的晚餐只供一人用。這位朋友(沒敢打擾牛頓)坐了下來匆匆把飯吃完。而牛頓從冥想中回到現實後，看着空空如也的盤碟，就說："嗯，真的，要不是因為證據就在眼前，我肯定敢發誓還沒吃過飯呢。"

——〔英〕穆爾

名人簡介

Isaac Newton（牛頓)(1642—1727)，英國物理學家、數學家和天文學家，提出萬有引力定律、力學三大定律、白光由色光組成的理論，並開創微積分等，著有《自然科學的數學原理》(*Philosophiae Naturalis Principia Mathematica*, 1687)、《光學》(*Opticks*, 1704)等。

16 His Accounts

Sir Isaac Newton, though so deep in Algebra and Fluxions, could not readily make up a common account; and, when he was Master of the Mint, used to get somebody to make up his accounts for him.

— *A. Pope*[1]

---

1. Alexander Pope (1688—1744)：蒲柏，英國詩人，長於諷刺，著有長篇諷刺詩《奪髮記》(*The Rape of the Lock*, 1712)等，翻譯了荷馬史詩《伊利亞特》(*Iliad*, 1715—20)和《奧德賽》(*Odyssey*, 1725—26)。

十六　不會做賬

儘管依撒克．牛頓爵士在代數學和流數領域有很深造詣，但卻不能輕鬆自如地結算普通的帳目。所以，當他擔任造幣廠廠長的時候，通常是找別人來替他做賬的。

——〔英〕蒲柏

名人簡介

Isaac Newton（牛頓）(1642—1727)，詳見第 15 篇。

17 The Anecdote of the Apple

The anecdote of the apple we learn from Voltaire[1], who had it from Newton's favourite niece, who with her husband lived and kept house for him all his later life. It is very like one of those anecdotes which are easily invented and believed in, and very often turn out on scrutiny to have no foundation. Fortunately this anecdote is well authenticated, and moreover is intrinsically probable; I say fortunately, because it is always painful to have to give up these child-learnt anecdotes,... This anecdote of the apple we need not resign. The tree was blown down in 1820 and part of its wood is preserved.

— *O. J. Lodge*[2]

---

1. Voltaire：伏爾泰，詳見第 4 篇。
2. O. J. Lodge：洛奇，詳見第 2 篇的註釋。

十七　蘋果趣事

這件有關蘋果的軼事，我們是從伏爾泰那兒聽來的，他又是從牛頓鍾愛的侄女那兒聽來的。這位侄女和她的丈夫陪伴牛頓度過晚年，並且替他料理家務。這件軼事極似那些隨意編造而且人們信以為真、可是一旦追根問底卻是毫無根據的軼聞故事。幸而這則趣事的可靠性是經過證實的。而且就其本身而言也是可能發生的。我之所以用幸而這個詞，是因為這些孩提時期就聽到的軼聞趣事，最後不得不割愛總是令人心痛的……。這則蘋果的趣聞，我們不必拋棄。那株蘋果樹在1820年被風颳倒，而一部分樹幹還保留至今。

——〔英〕洛奇

名人簡介

Isaac Newton（牛頓）(1642—1727)，詳見第 15 篇。

18 The Key to Muscle Action

One evening in the late eighteenth century an Italian woman stood in her kitchen watching the frogs' legs which she was preparing for the evening meal. "Look at those muscles moving. ... They always seem to come alive when I hang them on the copper wire."

Her husband [Luigi Galvani] looked... . The cut end of the frog's nerve was in contact with the copper wire, and electric current produced by the contact was passing along the nerve to the muscle. As a result, the muscle was twitching and contracting. ...

He had discovered the key to electricity, and to nerve conduction, and to muscle action. Here was the basis of all animal movement, reflex and voluntary, in frog and man.

— *W. Penfield*[1]

---

1. Wilder Graves Penfield (1891— 1976) ： 彭菲爾德，加拿大精神病學家， Montreal Neurological Institute 的創建人，創造癲癇病手術治療法。

十八　奧祕何在

十八世紀後期，一天晚上，一位意大利婦女站在她的廚房裏，觀察正用於做晚飯的青蛙腿。“瞧那些在顫動的肌肉。……每次我把腿掛在銅絲上的時候，這些腿總像是又變活了。”

她的丈夫〔伽伐尼〕看了看。……青蛙被切斷的神經末端與銅絲接觸，接觸產生的電流通過神經傳遞到肌肉組織。結果便引起了肌肉抽動和收縮。……

他發現了電的奧祕，發現了神經感應傳導的奧祕，發現了肌肉活動的奧祕。這便是動物的各種運動（包括反射運動和隨意運動）的基礎所在，青蛙和人都是這樣。

——*〔加拿大〕彭菲爾德*

名人簡介

Luigi Galvani（伽伐尼）(1737—1798)，意大利解剖學家、生理學家，發現生物電現象。許多電學術語源於他的名字。

19 The Musical Life

At the age of nineteen, he was thus launched in England with an outfit of some French, Latin, and English, picked up by himself; some skill in playing the hautboy, the violin, and the organ, as taught by his father; ...

He lived as musical instructor to one or two militia bands in Yorkshire, and for three years we hear no more than this of him.... He next obtained the post of organist at Halifax; and some four or five years later he was invited to become organist at the Octagon chapel in Bath, and soon led the musical life of that then very fashionable place.

While at Bath he wrote many musical pieces — glees, anthems, chants, pieces for the harp, and an orchestral symphony. He taught a large number of pupils, and lived a hard and successful life. After fourteen hours or so spent in teaching and playing, he would retire at night to instruct his mind with a study of mathematics, optics, Italian, or Greek, in all of which he managed to make some progress. He also about this time fell in with some book on astronomy.

— O. J. Lodge[1]

---

1. O. J. Lodge：洛奇，詳見第 2 篇的註釋。

十九　音樂生涯

他十九歲那年，憑着自學的一點法語、拉丁語和英語，被送到英國。他還會玩一點雙簧管、小提琴和風琴，是父親教給他的。……

在約克郡，他給一兩個民兵樂隊作音樂指導，藉以謀生。有三年光景，我們對他情況所知，僅此而已。……後來他在哈利法克斯得到一份風琴師的工作。大約又過了四、五年，他應邀到巴思的八角教堂任風琴師，並且不久就開始了在那當時甚為時髦之地的音樂生涯。

他在巴思生活期間，創作了許多音樂作品——重唱曲、聖歌、頌歌、豎琴曲，及一部為樂隊而寫的交響樂。他給許多學生上課，生活艱苦，而很有成就。每天十四小時左右的授課和演奏工作結束後，晚上他總是休息，靜心地自學一點數學、光學、意大利語，或是希臘語。在這幾方面，他都取得了一些進步。也就是在這個時期，他偶然讀到一本有關天文學的書。

——〔英〕洛奇

名人簡介

Frederick William Herschel（赫歇爾）(1738—1822)，英國天文學家，行星天文學的創始人，生於德國，自幼受到音樂教育，又多年從事音樂工作。1781年他發現了天王星，此後便完全放棄了音樂，全身心投入天文學。

20 The Great Enjoyment

Though Charles[1] was only fourteen, he and Erasmus[2] often worked late into the night. Word of this, and the smell of the burning sulphur..., caused Charles's fellow students to nickname him "Gas".

It also earned him a public rebuke from the renowned educator, Dr. Samuel Butler, headmaster of the Royal Free Grammar School of Shrewsbury,... Dr. Butler exclaimed before the student body:

"Darwin, you are wasting your time on useless subjects. Stick to your Greek grammar and Latin literature. They are the unfailing marks of an English gentleman."

...

... [He] had graduated in theology only four months before with a Bachelor of Arts degree from Christ's College in Cambridge, Class of 1831. He had finished tenth in the

---

1. Charles：即 Charles Darwin（達爾文）。
2. Erasmus：達爾文的哥哥，後來是醫生。

二十　魂之所繫

達爾文雖然只有十四歲，但和他哥哥伊拉茲馬斯常常工作到深夜。這方面的傳聞，還有硫黃燃燒味……，引得同學們給他起了個綽號叫“毒氣”。

這引起希魯茲伯里中學校長、著名教育家布特勒博士的當眾指責。……布特勒博士當着全班學生大聲說：

“達爾文，你把時間浪費在沒用的事情上。你要堅持學好希臘語法和拉丁文學。這些才是英國紳士永恆的標誌。”

……

……只是四個月前，他在劍橋大學基督學院1831年度神學專業班畢業，獲文學士學位。他畢業時被列入合格人

名人簡介

Charles Robert Darwin（查爾斯·達爾文）(1809—1882)，英國博物學家、進化論的創始人、進化生物學的奠基人，著有《物種起源》(*The Origin of Species*, 1859)、《人類的起源及性的選擇》(*The Descent of Man and Selection in Relation to Sex*, 1871)等。他在青少年時期就對大自然界充滿好奇心。他父親希望他繼承父業，也當醫生，曾送他去學醫。但他對醫學不感興趣，又被轉送學神學。然而他對神學也無興趣，卻熱衷於研究博物學。他後來回憶在劍橋捕捉昆蟲的往事時，認為採集昆蟲預示了後來的成功。本篇涉及達爾文中學時代和大學畢業時的情況。

list of successful candidates ... and would be ordained in the cathedral at Hereford, not far from where the Darwins and his relatives, the Wedgwoods, had their homes.

... The position of deacon or curate was at the bottom of the ecclesiastical ladder; ... If the duties of a curate were modest, and the pay equally so, Charles did not mind. The light job of work would leave him free for his collecting and pursuing of the natural histories, along with hunting, which he adored, the great enjoyment of his life.

— *I. Stone*[3]

3. Irving Stone (1903－1989)：斯通，美國傳記文學作家，擅長以歷史名人真實經歷為素材，創作其自稱的"傳記體小說"。 主要作品有荷蘭畫家Van Gogh傳《渴望生活》(*Lust for Life*, 1934)、美國作家Jack London傳《馬背上的水手》(*Sailor on Horseback*, 1938)等。本篇選自他主要作品之一達爾文傳《起源》(*The Origin*, 1975—80)。

選名單，排在第十位……。他將被分派到赫里福德大教堂任聖職。離達爾文一家和親屬韋奇伍德一家的住所不遠。

……執事或牧師助手這個職位是教會聖職階梯最低的一級。……如果說牧師助手的職責低微，那麼報酬也是這樣。達爾文並不在乎。輕鬆的工作使他有時間邊打獵，邊採集及研究自然歷史。這些是他喜歡做的事情，是他人生的一大樂趣。

——〔美〕斯通

21 Under the Shadow of Huxley

Here I was under the shadow of Huxley[1], ... I had been assigned to his course in Elementary Biology and afterwards I was to go on with Zoology under him.

...

... Huxley himself lectured in the little lecture theatre adjacent to the laboratory,... As I knew Huxley he was a yellow-faced, square-faced old man, with bright little brown eyes, lurking as it were in caves under his heavy grey eyebrows, and a mane of grey hair brushed back from his wall of forehead. He lectured in a clear firm voice without hurry and without delay, turning to the blackboard behind him to sketch some diagram, and always dusting the chalk from his fingers rather fastidiously before he resumed.... At the back of the auditorium were curtains, giving upon a museum devoted to the invertebrata. I was told that while Huxley lectured Charles Darwin[2] had been wont at times to come through those very curtains from the gallery behind

---

1. under...Huxley：此篇中，作者威爾斯回憶在師範學院進修生物學時，曾親自聆聽赫胥黎講課。
2. Charles Darwin：達爾文，詳見第 20 篇。

二十一　名師

這裏我受到赫胥黎的教誨，……我被指定聽他講授的基礎生物學課程，之後繼續聽他的動物學課。

……

……赫胥黎親自在一個與實驗室連接的小教室裏上課，……我認識的赫胥黎，是一位方型臉、黃膚色的老者，一雙棕色閃亮的小眼睛好像躲藏在他灰白的濃眉下的洞穴裏。密密的灰白長髮從前額梳向腦後。他講起課來，說話明確肯定，不緊不慢，時而轉向背後的黑板畫個圖解，總要把手上的粉筆灰撣得乾乾淨淨才接着講課。……教室的後部掛着簾子，通向無脊椎動物陳列室。別人告訴我，赫胥黎講課的時候，查爾斯．達爾文常從後面的陳列室走過

名人簡介

Thomas Henry Huxley（赫胥黎)(1825－1895)，英國博物學家、教育改革家，支持達爾文學說，第一個提出人類起源問題，著有《人在自然界中的地位》(*Evidence as to Man's Place in Nature*, 1863)、《進化論與倫理學》(*Evolution and Ethics*, 1893)等。

and sit and listen until his friend and ally had done. In my time Darwin had been dead for only a year or so (he died in 1882).

— *H. G. Wells*[3]

3. H.G. Wells：威爾斯，詳見第 51 篇。

簾子來，坐下聽課，一直聽到他的同行老友講完課。我在那裏上學時，達爾文去世只不過一年光景（他在 1882年去世）。

——〔英〕*威爾斯*

22 The Best Answer

The room they had entered had a tall mirror standing in one corner. Dodgson[1] gave his cousin an orange and asked her which hand she held it in. When she replied, "The right," he asked her to stand before the glass and tell him in which hand the little girl in the mirror was holding it. "The left hand," came the puzzled reply. "Exactly," said Dodgson, "and how do you explain that?" Alice Raikes did her best: "If I was on the other side of the glass," she said, "wouldn't the orange still be in my right hand?" Years later she remembered his laugh. "Well done, little Alice," he said. "The best answer I've had yet."

— *A. Raikes*[2]

1. Dodgson：筆名 Lewis Carroll（卡羅爾）。
2. Alice Raikes：艾麗絲・雷克斯，卡羅爾的小表妹。

二十二　最佳答案

在他們進來的這間房間的一角，立着一面高大的鏡子。道奇森給了表妹一個橘子，並且問她，她是用哪隻手拿着這個橘子。表妹回答："用右手。"這時，他讓她站到鏡子前，然後又要她說，鏡子裏的那個小姑娘用哪隻拿着橘子。"用左手啊，"表妹疑惑地答道。"完全正確，"道奇森說，"那麼，你怎麼解釋這個情況呢？"艾麗絲·雷克斯盡了最大的努力說："如果我站在鏡子的反面，橘子不是還該在我的右手嗎？"多年以後，她仍舊記得道奇森的笑聲。"回答得漂亮，小艾麗絲，"他說，"這是我到目前為止得到的最佳答案。"

——〔英〕雷克斯

名人簡介

Lewis Carroll（卡羅爾）(1832—1898)，真名 Charles Lutwidge Dodgson（道奇森），英國兒童文學作家、數學家。他所著《艾麗絲漫遊奇境記》(*Alice's Adventures in Wonderland*, 1865)享譽世界。

23 Interested in Everything

One day while Mr. Edison and I were calling on Luther Burbank in California, he asked us to register in his guest book. The book had a column for signature, another for home address, another for occupation and a final one entitled[1] "Interested in". Mr. Edison signed in a few quick but unhurried motions.... In the final column he wrote without an instant's[2] hesitation: "Everything".

— H. Ford[3]

---

1. entitled：to entitle = 給(書、文章等)題名。
2. instant：瞬息。
3. Henry Ford (1863 — 1947)：亨利·福特，美國汽車實業家，1903年創辦福特汽車公司，發明裝配綫生產法，促使美國成為汽車大國。

二十三　愛好一切

一天，我和愛迪生先生拜訪住在加利福尼亞州的盧瑟·伯班克。主人讓我們在會客簿上登記。會客簿有一欄供簽名用，另一欄用於填寫家庭地址，還有一欄作填寫職業用。最後一欄是"興趣愛好"。愛迪生先生快捷卻不失從容地，幾筆就簽完了名。……而在最後一欄裏，他則毫不遲疑地填上："一切"。

——〔美〕福特

名人簡介

Thomas Edison(愛迪生)(1847—1931)，美國自學成才的大發明家，十二歲當報童，後做電報員，依靠自己的力量從事實驗和發明，一生勤奮，獲得白熾燈、留聲機、話筒、電影機等發明專利達一千餘項。

24 Heavy Water

A letter...asked me whilst in Berkeley[1] to purchase or steal a gallon or so of heavy water, since it was needed desperately for dozens of experiments. He added kindly that Rutherford would willingly spend some money on it. So I collected about a gallon of 2 percent D_2O and paid $10 for it. After passing through the Customs with difficulty, since they did not understand why I should be importing a liquid which looked very like water, I presented the heavy water and the bill personally to Rutherford, only to find that he considered the price to be too high and I should have asked his authority for purchasing it.

— *J. D. Cockcroft*[2]

---

1. Berkeley：伯克利，美國港市。考克饒夫當時在美國訪問。
2. John Douglas Cockcroft (1897 — 1967)：考克饒夫，英國物理學家，因研究原子核的成就獲1951年諾貝爾物理學獎。他曾在盧瑟福（Rutherford）領導下工作。

二十四　重水

我在伯克利期間，收到一封信，……讓我去買，要不就偷一加侖左右的重水，因為有許多實驗都非常需要用重水。他在信中還好心地補充說，盧瑟福會很樂意為此事出些錢的。於是我收集了大約一加侖百分之二濃度的D_2O，為此支付了十美元。過海關的時候有些麻煩，因為海關人員弄不懂我為什麼要帶這種看上去很像水的液體入境。之後，我把重水和賬單親自交給盧瑟福，卻發現他認為這個價格太貴，而且我本該徵得他的同意後才可購買。

——〔英〕考克饒夫

名人簡介

Ernest Rutherford（盧瑟福）(1871－1937)，英國物理學家，因對元素衰變的研究獲 1908 年諾貝爾化學獎。

25 He Broke His Silence

As he was a late talker, his parents were worried. At last, at the supper table one night, he broke his silence to say, "The soup is too hot." Greatly relieved, his parents asked why he had never said a word before. Albert replied, "Because up to now everything was in order."

— *Otto Neugebauer*[1]

1. Otto Neugebauer：諾伊格包爾，德國古代數學的歷史學家。

二十五　打破沉默

由於他開口說話較遲，他的父母很擔憂。終於有一天，在晚餐桌旁，他不再保持沉默，開口說道，“湯太燙了。”他的父母總算大大鬆了一口氣，便問為什麼以前他總是一言不發。阿爾伯特答道，“因為直到目前為止，一切都正常呀。”

—〔德〕諾伊格包爾

名人簡介

Albert Einstein（阿爾伯特．愛因斯坦）(1879—1955)，美籍德國理論物理學家，創立“相對論”，獲 1921 年諾貝爾物理學獎。

Poets & Writers
詩人和作家

26 A Banquet Made of Tongues

His Master, Xantus, who was giving a banquet for his friends, ordered him one day to compose a meal of the best ingredients he could buy. Aesop served a banquet in which every dish, from the soup to the dessert, was made of tongues prepared in various ways. When Xantus reproved him, Aesop replied that he had followed his orders to the letter, since the tongue being the organ of language, is also the vehicle of truth, reason, science, social life and all things that make life precious. The next day Xantus ordered Aesop to prepare a meal consisting of all the worst ingredients. Aesop again served the same dishes, explaining that the tongue, as the organ of language, is also responsible for all the worst things in the world — quarrels, dissensions, lawsuits, strife, war, lies, slander, blasphemy and all manner of things evil.

— *G. Apollinaire*[1]

1. Guillaume Apollinaire (1880—1918)：阿波里耐，法國現代主義詩人，主張革新詩歌，代表作為《醇酒集》(*Alcools*, 1913)。

二十六　舌宴

一天，他的主人安特斯要宴請朋友，便命令伊索用買得到的最佳材料準備一頓飯菜。結果伊索為宴會上的每一道菜，從湯到甜點，都是用舌頭經各種方法烹調而成的。當安特斯訓斥他的時候，伊索回答說，他是不折不扣地執行了主人的命令。因為舌頭作為語言器官，也是真理、理性、科學、社交和使生活變得珍貴的一切事物的載體。第二天，安特斯又命令伊索用所有最蹩腳的配料準備一頓飯菜。伊索還是上了同樣的菜肴，並解釋道，舌頭作為語言器官，也導致了世上最壞的事情——爭吵、不和、官司、衝突、戰爭、謊言、誹謗、褻瀆和各種各樣的罪孽。

——〔法〕阿波里耐

名人簡介

Aesop（伊索）(公元前約620—約560)，古希臘寓言作家，相傳曾為奴隸，善講寓言故事，經後人匯編成《伊索寓言》(*Aesop's Fables*)。

27 A Desire of Knowledge

On Saturday, July 30, Dr. Johnson and I took a sculler ...and set out for Greenwich[1]. I asked him if he really thought a knowledge of the Greek and Latin languages an essential requisite to a good education. Johnson: "Most certainly, Sir; for those who know them have a very great advantage over those who do not. Nay, Sir, it is wonderful what a difference learning makes upon people even in the common intercourse of life, which does not appear to be much connected with it." — "And yet," said I, "people go through the world very well, and carry on the business of life to good advantage, without learning." Johnson: "Why, Sir, that may be true in cases where learning cannot possibly be of any use; for instance, this boy rows us as well without learning,..." He then called to the boy, "What would you give, my lad, to know about the Argonauts[2]?" "Sir," said the boy, "I would give what I have."

---

1. Greenwich：格林尼治，英國城市，位於倫敦東南，泰晤士河畔，本初子午綫經過這裏。
2. Argonauts：希臘神話中乘阿爾戈號快船去海外覓取金羊毛的英雄。

二十七　求知慾

七月三十日，星期六那天，我和約翰遜乘上小船出發到格林尼治去。我問他是否真的認為通曉希臘文和拉丁文是良好教育必不可少的條件。約翰遜說："當然是的，先生。因為通曉這兩種語言的人大大優勝於那些不懂這兩種語言的人。不僅如此，先生，即使在與學問似乎沒有很大關係的日常生活交往中，學問使人產生的差異真是太大了。"——我說："不過，沒有學問，人們照樣度過人生，並且活得很好。"約翰遜說："哦，先生，在那些知識用不到的情況下，也許是這樣的。譬如說，這個男孩沒有學問也能為我們把船划得很好，……"接着他對划槳人說："小夥子，為了知道阿爾戈英雄的故事，你願意付出什麼代價？"那個男孩說："我願拿出我所有的一切。"約翰遜對

名人簡介

Samuel Johnson（約翰遜）(1709—1784)，英國作家、評論家、辭書編纂者。他曾被當時評論家譽為英國"文壇泰斗"。1747 年他發表英語詞典 (*A Dictionary of the English Language*) 的編寫計劃。1755 年詞典問世，為他贏得聲譽，後人編的英語詞典無不以此為基礎。他於1763年創立 Literary Club，吸納當時不少重要名人。

Johnson was much pleased with his answer, and we gave him a double fare. Dr. Johnson then turning to me, "Sir," said he, "a desire of knowledge is the natural feeling of mankind; and every human being, whose mind is not debauched, will be willing to give all that he has to get knowledge."

— *J. Boswell*[3]

3. James Boswell (1740—1795)：鮑斯韋爾，英國作家，所著 *Life of Dr. Samuel Johnson* 獲得很高聲譽。本篇軼事即選自該書。關於 Boswell，詳見他的軼事"A Vow"（第29篇）。

他的回答十分滿意。於是，我們付了他雙倍的船費。然後，約翰遜轉過身來對我說：“先生，求知慾是人類的本性。凡是不墮落的人都願意為獲取知識付出一切。”

——〔英〕鮑斯韋爾

28 Arrested by His Landlady

I received one morning a message from poor Goldsmith that he was in great distress, and it was not in his power to come to me, begging that I would come to him as soon as possible. I sent him a guinea[1] and promised to come to him directly. I accordingly went as soon as I was dressed, and found that his landlady had arrested him for his rent, at which[2] he was in a violent passion. I perceived that he had already changed my guinea, and had got a bottle of Madeira. I began to talk to him of the means by which he might be extricated. He then told me that he had a novel ready for the press, which he produced to me. I looked into it, and saw its merit; told the landlady I should soon return, and, having gone to a bookseller, sold it for sixty pounds. I brought Goldsmith the money, and he discharged his rent, not without grating his landlady in a high tone for having used him so ill.

— *S. Johnson*[3]

---

1. guinea：舊英國金幣名。
2. which：指前句中所言，即被房東拘禁一事。
3. Samuel Johnson：約翰遜，詳見第 27 篇。

二十八　遭受拘禁

一天早晨，可憐的哥爾德斯密斯給我捎來口信，說他正遭受危難，身不由己，無法來看我，乞求我去看他，愈快愈好。我給他送去一個金幣，答應即刻就到他那兒去。為此，我一穿戴完畢就去了。原來是這麼回事：他的女房東因房租問題把他拘禁起來了。哥爾德斯密斯為此而大發雷霆。我注意到他已把我給他的那個金幣換成了零錢，買了一瓶馬德拉白葡萄酒。我開始和他商討脫身之計。這時候他告訴我，他有部小說已經脫稿，可以付印，便拿出來給我看。我翻閱了一遍，發現了書的價值，便告訴房東我一會就回來。我去找了個書商，把小說賣了，換得六十英鎊。我把稿酬帶回給哥爾德斯密斯。他便償清了房租，對於女房東這樣虐待他，少不了敞開嗓門破口大罵。

——〔英〕約翰遜

名人簡介

Oliver Goldsmith (1730—1774)：哥爾德斯密斯，英國詩人、劇作家、小說家，主要著作有小說《威克菲爾德的牧師》(*The Vicar of Wakefield*, 1766)、長詩《荒村》(*The Deserted Village*, 1770)等。

29 A Vow

Boswell's career was completely dominated by his innate characteristics.... At the age of twenty-three he discovered Dr. Johnson[1]. A year later he was writing to him, at Wittenberg[2], "from the tomb of Melancthon[3]": "My paper rests upon the gravestone of that great and good man.... At this tomb, then, my ever dear and respected friend! I vow to thee an eternal attachment." The rest of Boswell's existence was the history of that vow's accomplishment.

...

...With incredible persistence he had carried through the enormous task which he had set himself thirty years earlier. Everything else was gone. He was burnt down to the wick, but his work was there.

— *L. Strachey*[4]

---

1. Dr. Johnson：即Samuel Johnson (約翰遜)，詳見第 27 篇。
2. Wittenberg：維丁堡，德國城市，位於易北河中游。
3. Melancthon (1497—1560)：梅蘭希頓，德國學者、宗教改革家、教育家。
4. Lytton Strachey (1880 — 1932)：斯特雷奇，英國傳記作家、評論家，以所著《維多利亞女王時代名人傳》(*Eminent Victorians*, 1918)和《維多利亞女王傳》(*Queen Victoria*, 1921)而聞名。他把寫傳記看成創作藝術作品。

二十九　誓言

鮑斯韋爾的事業完全由他天生的性格決定。……他在二十三歲的時候發現了約翰遜博士。一年以後，他在維丁堡的梅蘭希頓墳墓上給約翰遜寫信，他寫道："我的紙放在這位偉大的好心人墓碑上。……那麼，在墓前，我最敬愛的朋友！我向你發誓，我要成為你的忠實朋友，將終生不渝。"鮑斯韋爾的一生就是實現這個誓言的歷史。

……

……他以驚人的毅力完成了在三十年前為自己確定的重大任務。其他一切都已煙消雲散。他的生命已燃盡，但是他的作品永存不朽。

——〔英〕斯特雷奇

名人簡介

James Boswell（鮑斯韋爾）(1740—1795)，英國作家，所著 *Life of Dr. Samuel Johnson* (1791)獲得很高聲譽。他於1763年在倫敦遇見約翰遜(Johnson)，1772 至 1784 年期間，經常拜訪約翰遜。1773年和約翰遜同遊英國赫布里底群島，在和約翰遜交往中不斷地筆錄他的談話。約翰遜的聲譽頗得力於鮑斯韋爾為他寫的傳記。

30 The Young Werther

Then three new characters were born: Werther, Charlotte, and Albert[1]. Werther was Goethe if he had not been an artist. Albert was a slightly meaner Kestner....

On the following day he shut himself up to work, and in four weeks the book was written.

When Goethe had finished *The Sorrows of the Young Werther* he felt as free and happy as after a general confession....

...

As soon as he had received the first volumes from the printer, he packed up two copies, one for Charlotte and one for Kestner, and wrote to Lotte: "You will realize when you read this book how dear it is to me; and this copy above all I value as much as if it were the only one in the world. It is for

---

1. Werther, Charlotte, and Albert：歌德名著《少年維特之煩惱》中的人物名。維特 (Werther) 是個能詩善畫的青年，深深地愛上年輕活潑的姑娘綠蒂 (Charlotte，又名 Lotte)，但她已經是青年阿爾貝 (Albert) 的未婚妻。該書情節以作者的經歷為基礎，小說中的綠蒂與現實中作者熱戀過的綠蒂同名，阿爾貝的原型是綠蒂的男友 Kestner。

三十　少年維特

三個新人物便產生了：維特、綠蒂和阿爾貝。維特就是歌德，不同的是，維特是個畫家。阿爾貝的才氣比起凱斯納稍遜一籌。……

第二天，他閉門寫作，四星期後，全書寫成。

當歌德寫完《少年維特之煩惱》的時候，他的感覺就像懺悔了一切以後那樣輕鬆愉快。……

……

他從出版商手中拿到第一批書後，便立即包裝了兩本書，一本給綠蒂，另一本給凱斯納。他給綠蒂寫道："當你讀這本書的時候，你會覺得這本書對我來說是多麼珍貴。我尤其把這本書看作世界上獨一無二的珍寶。這本書是給

名人簡介

Johann Wolfgang von Goethe（歌德）(1749—1832)，德國詩人、劇作家、小說家，德國古典文學和民族文學的主要代表。18 世紀德國文學的成就與歌德的名字分不開。他在文學、藝術、自然科學、哲學、歷史學、政治等領域均有卓著的成就。代表作有詩劇《浮士德》(*Faust*, 1808—32)、小說《少年維特之煩惱》(*The Sorrows of the Young Werther*, 1774)等。後者是德國文學第一部對世界產生重大影響的作品，我國早在20世紀初已有介紹。

you, Lotte. I have kissed it a hundred times, and I kept it shut up so that no one might touch it. Oh, Lotte, I want each of you to read it by yourselves and separately. You by yourself and Kestner by himself, and then I want each of you to write me a line. Lotte — good-bye, Lotte."

— *A. Maurois*[2]

---

2. André Maurois (1885 — 1967)：莫洛亞，法國作家，原名 Emile-Salomon-Wilhelm Herzog，作品有小說和歷史著作，尤以文學家傳記聞名，包括英國的拜倫、雪萊、法國的巴爾扎克、雨果、大仲馬、小仲馬等人的傳記。

你綠蒂的。我吻過它一百次，把書合上，不讓任何人碰它。哦，綠蒂，我要你們二人各自分開讀這本書。你一個人讀，凱斯納也一個人讀。你們讀完以後，分別給我寫句話。綠蒂——再見，綠蒂。”

——〔法〕莫洛亞

31 A Private Citizen

Goethe[1] dresses very simply, has already dispensed with toupet and curls, seldom goes to court, rarely appears in society. As minister[2] he lives like a private citizen, deliberately cultivates a stiff and formal manner, says little....

Goethe relies upon a high barometer, retires early and rises early, writes only in the morning, spends whole weeks in his summer-house, rides, skates, has his healthiest years between the ages of forty and fifty....

Goethe discharges his offices and his duties promptly in order to devote himself to study and writing.

— *E. Ludwig*[3]

1. Goethe：歌德是一位風雲人物，但從本篇軼事可看出，他也是一個簡樸的人。
2. As minister：1775 年，歌德應魏瑪公國 (Weimar) 的公爵邀請，擔任部長和樞密顧問，由於積極參與政事，從政的最初十年內創作稀少。
3. E. Ludwig：路德維格，詳見第 4 篇的註釋。

三十一　淡泊明志

那時歌德穿着很簡樸，已經不用假髮和捲髮，很少去宮廷，不常在社交場合露面。他是個部長，但生活像個平民百姓，刻意養成審慎拘謹的作風，很少說話。……

歌德信賴一個精密的氣壓計，早睡早起，只在上午寫作，連續幾個星期在避暑別墅裏度過，騎馬、滑冰，四十到五十歲是他健康最佳時期。……

歌德處理公務雷厲風行，以便騰出多些時間學習和寫作。

——〔德〕路德維格

名人簡介

Johann Wolfgang von Goethe（歌德）(1749－1832)，詳見第30篇。

32 An Unsought Wife

With a lonely home and two little girls to care for, Godwin thought once more of marriage. Twice his wooing was unsuccessful, and the philosopher who believed that reason was omnipotent, tried in vain in long, elaborate letters to argue two ladies into love. His second wife came unsought. As he sat one day at his window,... a handsome widow spoke to him from the neighbouring balcony, with these arresting words, "Is it possible that I behold the immortal Godwin?" They were married before the close of the year (1801).

Mrs Clairmont was a strange successor to Mary Wollstonecraft[1]. She was a vulgar and worldly woman, thoroughly feminine, and rather inclined to boast of her total ignorance of philosophy.

— *H. N. Brailsford*[2]

---

1. Mary Wollstonecraft Godwin (1759—1797)：戈德溫，英國女作家，於 1797 年與 William Godwin 結婚。他們所生的女兒在 1816 年與詩人雪萊(Shelley)結婚。
2. H. N. Brailsford：布雷斯福，英國人，*Shelley, Godwin, and Their Circle* 一書的作者。

三十二　送上門的妻子

寂寞的家和兩個還需照管的小女兒使戈德溫再一次想結婚。他兩次求愛未獲成功。這位視理智為萬能的哲學家想通過再三斟酌的長篇書信說服兩位女子投入情愛，卻以徒勞告終。他的第二位妻子得來毫不費力。一天，當他坐在自家窗前的時候，……隔壁陽台上，有一位長相俊秀的寡婦朝他說了一句引起他注意的話："我看見了長生不老的戈德溫，這可能嗎？"他們就在那年（1801年）底結了婚。

克萊爾蒙特太太繼瑪麗．沃爾斯通克拉夫特之後，是一位奇怪的夫人。她是個平庸俗氣的女人，女性十足。她對哲學一竅不通，卻往往喜歡以此炫耀。

——〔英〕布雷斯福

名人簡介

William Godwin（戈德溫）(1756—1836)，英國社會思想家、作家，代表作《有關政治正義之研究》(*An Enquiry Concerning Political Justice*, 1793)闡述了他改革社會的觀點，對19世紀初英國的進步思潮頗有影響，例如詩人雪萊就受到他很大的影響。

33 A High Officer

Schiller ... dresses with utmost care, orders the most expensive material for his evening clothes, keeps up a large house, at thirty-eight he has his coach and horses, ... In the first year of his marriage he cannot travel with his wife as far as Leipzig without valets and maids. He is brilliant in society, and in his court uniform with epaulettes he can be mistaken for a high officer by Madame de Stael[1]. ...

A man of genius, polished, interested in politics and esthetics, Schiller had several business men around him; and in his desire for power and money he would probably have taken this course had it not been for his illness and for Goethe[2]. Comrades of his youth picked him out for a diplomat; ...

— E. Ludwig[3]

---

1. Madame de Staël (1766—1817)：斯塔爾夫人，原名 Germaine Necker，法國女作家、文藝理論家，廣交文壇名流的沙龍主人。
2. Goethe：歌德，詳見第 30 篇。1794 年起，席勒和歌德開始合作，共同工作達十多年。
3. E. Ludwig：路德維格，詳見第 4 篇的註釋。

三十三　高級官員

席勒……對穿着極為講究，他定購最昂貴的衣料縫製晚禮服，住在一幢大房子裏。三十八歲時就有自己的馬車和馬匹，……在他婚姻生活的第一個年頭裏，他與妻子外出，即使只到來比錫也非帶男女僕從不可。他在上層社會中光彩照人。當他身着佩戴肩章的宮廷服裝時，會讓斯塔爾夫人錯認為高級官員。……

席勒有才華，有教養，對政治和美學頗感興趣，他身邊有幾個商人。如果不是因為有病，還由於歌德的緣故，出於對權力和金錢的慾望，他真會走上那條路。青年時代的同伴們認他為外交家。……

——〔德〕路德維格

名人簡介

Johann Friedrich von Schiller（席勒）(1759—1805)，德國詩人、劇作家、歷史學家、文藝理論家，在德國文學中佔有很重要的地位，主要作品有劇本《華倫斯坦》(*Wallenstein*, 1800)、《陰謀與愛情》(*Kabale und Liebe*, 1784)、《威廉・退爾》(*Wilhelm Tell*, 1804)等。

34 Disorder

Schiller, accustomed to learning more from books than from people, unused to life in the open, tubercular, and in constant fear of his attacks, passes much of his time indoors, never takes physical exercise, sits for whole weeks in summer in a closed room, smoking and taking snuff.

Usually sleepless at night, he can make no definite arrangements for the next day, sometimes does not have his luncheon until eight, on bad days must bolster up his strength with alcohol, and writes best when the barometer is low....

Schiller, who is often bewildered by the multitude of his enterprises, is completely prevented from working by sickness.... Schiller's outward[1] life is made more difficult by disorder,...

— *E. Ludwig*[2]

1. outward：肉體的，相對於“精神的”。
2. E. Ludwig：路德維格，詳見第 4 篇的註釋。

三十四　生活無律

席勒習慣於從書本學習，不習慣向人們學習，不習慣戶外生活。他患有結核病，總是害怕疾病會發作。因此，他的大部分時間是在室內度過的，從不運動。在夏季，他把自己關在房間裏，一坐就是幾個星期，既抽煙又吸鼻煙。

他晚間通常睡不着覺，對第二天不作明確的安排。他有時到晚上八點才吃午飯。如果遇到壞天氣，必需借助酒來提神。當氣壓計顯示低點的時候，他的寫作效果最佳。……

席勒從事多項工作，常常感到為難，更由於疾病纏身而完全不能工作。…… 起居無規律使席勒的生活更加困難了，……

——〔德〕路德維格

名人簡介

Johann Friedrich von Schiller（席勒）(1759—1805)，詳見第 33 篇。

35 Cupid[1] and Psyche[2]

Cupid is taking her [Psyche's] lovely chin, and turning her pouting mouth to meet his while he archly bends his own down, as if saying, "Pretty dear!" ... Catching sight of the Cupid, as he[3] and I were coming out, Wordsworth's face reddened, he showed his teeth and then said in a loud voice, "THE DEV-V-V-VILS!"

— *B. Haydon*[4]

---

1. Cupid：丘比特，羅馬愛神。此處指他的雕塑。
2. Psyche：普賽克，希臘和羅馬的神，以少女形象出現的人類靈魂的化身。此處指她的雕塑。
3. he：指 William Wordsworth（華茲華斯）。
4. Benjamin Robert Haydon (1786—1846)：海頓，英國畫家，以《聖經》和歷史題材的油畫著稱，著有 *Autobiography* (1847)。

三十五　丘比特與普賽克

丘比特正去托她（普賽克）可愛的下巴，躬背俯身，把她撅起的嘴轉過來觸到自己的雙唇上，似乎在說：“美人，親愛的！”…… 我和華茲華斯正準備出來時，他一眼看到了這座丘比特雕像便脹紅了臉，怒氣沖沖，接着便大聲嚷道：“魔── 鬼!”

──〔英〕海頓

名人簡介

William Wordsworth（華茲華斯）(1770—1850)，英國詩人，作品歌頌大自然，開創浪漫主義新詩風，主要作品有與 S. T. Coleridge 合寫的《抒情歌謠集》(*Lyrical Ballads*, 1798—1805)、長詩《序曲》(*The Prelude*, 1805)等，1843 年被封為桂冠詩人。

36 He Failed to Remove the Collar

I removed the harness...but...could not get off the collar. In despair I called for assistance. Mr. Wordsworth[1] first brought his ingenuity into exercise: he relinquished the achievement as altogether impracticable. Mr. Coleridge now tried his hand, but, after twisting the poor horse's neck almost to strangulation...he gave up the useless task, pronouncing that the horse's head must have grown (gout or dropsy!) since the collar was put on! For it was a downright impossibility for such a large *os frontis*[2] to pass through so narrow a collar! At about this juncture, the servant girl appeared, turned the collar upside down, and removed it.

— *J. Cottle*[3]

---

1. Mr. Wordsworth：華茲華斯，詳見第 35 篇。
2. *os frontis* ：〔拉丁語〕額骨。
3. Joseph Cottle (1770—1853)：考特爾，英國書商和詩人，他經手出版了 Southey 、 Coleridge 和 Wordsworth 等人的初期作品。

三十六　束手無策

我給馬卸馬具，……可是……卸不下馬軛。無望之中，只好請人幫忙。華茲華斯第一個使出了他的聰明才智，但因完全無望做到而作罷。接着柯爾律治先生來試身手。他把馬脖子扭得差點沒把可憐的馬憋死，……不見成效，只得作罷。他還說，馬軛戴上後，這馬的頭一定是長大了(痛風或是浮腫)，因為馬這麼大的額骨根本不可能穿過這麼窄小的馬軛！就在這時，年輕女僕來了，她把馬軛往下一翻，便脫了下來。

——〔英〕考特爾

名人簡介

Samuel Taylor Coleridge（柯爾律治）(1772—1834)，英國詩人、文學評論家，與華茲華斯（Wordsworth）合著《抒情歌謠集》，開創英國文學史上浪漫主義新時期，還有詩作《忽必烈汗》(*Kubla Khan*, 1816)、評論著作《文學傳記》(*Biographia Literaria*, 1817)等。

37 An Eloquent Discourse

He drew me within the door of an unoccupied garden by the roadside...took me by the button of my coat, and, closing his eyes, commenced an eloquent discourse, waving his right hand gently, as the musical words flowed in an unbroken stream from his lips...I saw that it was no use to attempt to break away, so taking advantage of his absorption in his subject, I, with my penknife, quietly severed the button from my coat, and decamped. Five hours afterwards, in passing the same garden, on my way home, I heard Coleridge's voice and, looking in, there he was, with closed eyes — the button in his fingers — and his right hand gracefully waving, just as when I left him.

— *C. Lamb*[1]

1. Charles Lamb (1775—1834)：蘭姆，英國散文家、文學評論家。他為朋友 Coleridge 的第一部詩集(1796)撰寫了四首十四行詩（sonnets），著有《莎士比亞故事集》(*Tales from Shakespeare*, 1807，與胞姐 Mary 合寫)、《伊利亞隨筆集》(*Essays of Elia*, 1823) 等。

三十七　滔滔不絕

他把我拉進路邊一座空置的花園門後……他拽着我衣服的一粒紐扣，閉着眼睛就開始滔滔不絕地講起來。隨着口中吐出一串串音樂般的話語，他輕柔地揮舞着右手……我知道無法脱身。於是，我趁他專注於演講的時候，用小刀悄悄地割下衣服上的扣子，溜之大吉了。五個小時後，我回家路經那座花園，聽到柯爾律治的聲音，朝裏邊一看，他還在那兒，閉着雙眼 —— 那顆紐扣還捏在手裏 —— 右手優美地揮舞着，就像我離開他時的樣子一樣。

——〔英〕*蘭姆*

名人簡介

Samuel Taylor Coleridge（柯爾律治）(1772—1834)，詳見第 36 篇。

38 Terror of Getting Fat

[His] terror of getting fat was so great that he reduced his diet to the point of absolute starvation. When he added to his weight, even standing was painful, so he resolved to keep down to eleven stone or shoot himself. He said everything he swallowed was instantly converted to tallow and deposited on his ribs. He was the only human being I ever met with who had sufficient self-restraint and resolution to resist his proneness to fatten. As he was always hungry, his merit was the greater. Occasionally he relaxed his vigilance, when he swelled apace. I remember one of his old friends saying, "Byron, how well you are looking!" If he had stopped there it had been well, but when he added, "You are getting fat," Byron's brow reddened, and his eye flashed — "Do you call getting fat looking well, as if I were a hog?" and turning to me he muttered, "The beast, I can hardly keep my hands off him."

— *E. J. Trelawney*[1]

---

1. Edward John Trelawney (1792—1881)：特里勞尼，英國作家和冒險家，與雪萊和拜倫過從甚密，曾隨拜倫投身希臘民族獨立鬥爭，著有《幼子奇遇》(*Adventures of a Younger Son*, 1831)、《雪萊、拜倫和我》(*Records of Shelley, Byron and the Author*, 1878)等。

三十八　肥胖

他對發胖非常恐懼，以致把飲食量減少到完全挨餓的地步。當體重有所增加時，哪怕站着他也會痛苦不堪，所以他決意要把體重降到十一呃，否則就開槍了結自己。他說他所吞下的全部食物都會馬上變成脂肪，儲存在肋骨上。要是有誰有足夠的自我克制力並決心抵禦不斷肥胖，那他是我遇見到的唯一的一個人了。由於他總是處於飢餓狀態，他減肥的效果甚好。偶爾，他放鬆警惕。這時，他就會很快發胖。我記得他的一位老朋友說："拜倫，你看上去真不錯！"如果他的話到此為止就好了，可他接着說："你在發胖了。"這時，拜倫的臉色變得通紅，眼睛裏閃着光，說："你把發胖也說成好看，看來我就像頭公豬啦？"說罷轉過身來對我嘟噥道："這畜生，我可不會放過他。"

——〔英〕特里勞尼

名人簡介

George Gordon Byron（拜倫）(1788—1824)，英國詩人，詩路寬廣，擅長諷刺，在投身希臘民族獨立戰爭中病逝，代表作有《恰爾德．哈羅爾德遊記》(*Childe Harold's Pilgrimage*, 1812)、《唐璜》(*Don Juan*, 1819)等。

39 Asleep in the Daytime

He would often fall asleep in the daytime — dropping off in a moment — like an infant. He often quietly transferred himself from his chair to the floor, and slept soundly on the carpet, and in the winter upon the rug, basking in the warmth like a cat; and like a cat his little round head was roasted before a blazing fire....

— *T. J. Hogg*[1]

1. Thomas Jefferson Hogg (1792—1862)：霍格，英國法學家和作家，雪萊最好的朋友，著有 *Life of Shelley* (1858)。

三十九 嗜睡

他經常在白天打瞌睡，像嬰兒似的，説睡就睡。他常常不聲不響地從椅子上轉移到地上，在地毯上呼呼大睡起來。冬天他睡在地毯上，溫暖舒適像隻貓，他讓那小圓腦袋也像貓那樣，在旺盛的爐火前烘烤着。……

——〔英〕*霍格*

名人簡介

Percy Bysshe Shelley（雪萊）(1792—1822)，英國浪漫主義詩人，主要作品有長詩《伊斯蘭的反叛》(*Revolt of Islam*, 1817)、詩劇《解放了的普羅米修斯》(*Prometheus Unbound*, 1820)、抒情詩《西風頌》(*Ode to the West Wind*, 1819)等。本篇選段描述他如飢似渴，日以繼夜地大量閱讀的生活習慣。

40 He Read Like a Madman

Inspired by the remarkable changes in the social structure caused by the Revolution[1], the youth[2] sought to escape from the narrow confines and the bleakness of his home. He found life at school in Vendôme[3] very strict. He had to stay after class, was beaten, and was even put in confinement; but there happened to be an old priest here in charge of the library who gave him access to all the books. The boy, whose childhood had brought him nothing, now began reading, and he read steadily for the next three years. He read like a madman, greedily and haphazardly — and at the age of twelve he wrote a treatise on the human will. But this overstimulation of the brain proved too much for him. He was brought home suffering from fever and prostration, and lay for weeks in a state of semi-consciousness.

---

1. the Revolution：即 the French Revolution (1789－1794)，法國大革命。
2. the youth：指 Honoré de Balzac（巴爾扎克）。
3. Vendôme：旺多姆，1907年巴爾扎克進入該地寄宿學校。這學校制度古板，教師冷漠殘酷。

四十　廢寢忘食

革命引起社會結構的深刻變化。這個青年受此鼓舞，設法跳出狹隘的圈子和乏味的家庭。他發現旺多姆學校的生活非常嚴厲。上完課後，他得留下來，挨打，甚至被關禁。然而學校裏卻有一位老牧師掌管着圖書館。這個牧師容許他使用館內全部圖書。這個在童年時代毫無所得的孩子從那時起開始閱讀，在以後的三年中堅持不懈。他讀起書來如癡如狂，飢不擇食，見書就讀。他十二歲時就寫了一篇關於人類意志的專題論文。然而，這對腦力過度刺激，超過了他的承受力。他因發燒和虛脱被送回家。他神志處於半昏迷狀態，臥牀不起，足有好幾週。

名人簡介

Honoré de Balzac（巴爾扎克）(1799—1850)，法國小説家，法國現實主義小説的奠基人。他創作之多實屬罕見，代表作《驢皮記》(1831)、《歐也妮．葛朗台》(1833)、《高老頭》(1834)等都是大家熟悉的。其巨著《人間喜劇》（*The Human Comedy*）包括小説 91 部，反映了法國的社會變革和人情風俗。他童年不幸，未嘗到家庭的溫暖。本篇描述他雖處學校沉悶窒息的環境，卻在書籍王國裏尋找樂趣。

... at the age of twenty, after a second school period at Paris, where he read omnivorously while studying law, he definitely decided to become an author.

— *E. Ludwig*[4]

---

4. E. Ludwig：路德維格，詳見第 4 篇的註釋。

……他二十歲時，在巴黎攻讀法律的同時，博覽群書。這第二期的求學以後，他斷然決定當個作家。

——*〔德〕路德維格*

41 In Excessive Labour

I must tell you that I am submerged in excessive labour. The mechanics of my life have altered. I go to bed at six or seven in the evening, like the hens. I am awakened at one o'clock in the morning and work till eight. At eight I sleep for an hour and a half. Then I have something light to eat, and a cup of black coffee, and harness my wagon until four. I receive callers, I take a bath or go out, and after dinner I go back to bed. I have to live like this for months on end if I am not to be overwhelmed by my obligations. The profits accrue slowly; the debts are inexorable and fixed. It is now certain that I shall make a great fortune; but I need to go on writing and working for another three years.

— *Balzac*

四十一　極度勞碌

我必須告訴你們，我已陷入極度的勞碌之中。我的生活規律改變了。每天像母雞一樣，傍晚六、七點鐘就上牀，半夜一點讓人叫醒，工作到上午八點。接着又是一個半小時的睡眠之後，稍吃一點東西，喝一杯清咖啡。然後再拚命幹到下午四點。這時候我會客、洗澡或外出。我吃過晚飯再睡覺。要是我不被這些事務壓垮的話，我得像這樣連續幹上好幾個月。收益增長緩慢，而債務是無情的、不容更改的。現在可以肯定，我會發大財的。不過我還須苦幹三年，不斷寫作。

——〔法〕巴爾扎克

名人簡介

Honoré de Balzac（巴爾扎克）(1799—1850)，詳見第 40 篇。

42 My Moral Sun

Once in his life[1], and only once, he experienced love simply, without romanticism or affectation, ...

Madame de Berny[2], ... lived with an old partially blind husband and nine children on their charming estate where Balzac came, at the age of twenty-three, to visit his friend, her son. ... Her features, ...were certain to captivate the youth, especially since he found here for the first time a woman of education, tact and breeding, who belonged to those circles which vaguely troubled the little provincial.

First she refused him, then she acquiesced. ...

This woman raised and educated Balzac, backing him in business and in failure with money and sound advice. From the nature of his devotion, she foresaw his talent, and for twenty years she gave him the advantage of her prudent and

---

1. Once in his life：巴爾扎克（Balzac）勤奮一生，創作了大量的文學財富，卻過了一輩子獨身生活。1850 年 3 月他到烏克蘭與一俄國貴婦結婚。這時，他已身心交瘁，健康每況愈下，5 月返回巴黎後，便臥牀不起，同年 8 月去世。
2. Madame de Berny：這位貴族婦人比巴爾扎克大 22 歲，既賢惠又有才能。她敢於衝破世俗的羈絆，對巴爾扎克體貼入微，關懷備至，使巴爾扎克感受到從小沒領略過的母愛般的溫情。

四十二　心靈的太陽

在他的一生中有過一次，只有一次，純真地感受了愛情，不風流，不裝模作樣，……

貝爾尼夫人……與她年老的、部分失明的丈夫，還有九個孩子生活在一個美麗的莊園裏。這個莊園巴爾扎克曾經到過。當時他二十三歲，他去拜訪一位朋友，就是貝爾尼夫人的兒子。……她的容貌，……無疑打動了這位年青人的心，特別是因為他在這裏第一次發現有一位受過教育、舉止得體、有教養的女人。她屬於那些使這個外省小人物隱約地感到煩惱的階層的人。

起初巴爾扎克被她拒絕，後來她也就默認了。……

這位婦女提攜並教育巴爾扎克，以經濟資助和忠告扶持他的事業，幫他度過難關。她獨具慧眼，從巴爾扎克專心致志的本性預見到他的才能。二十年中，她發揮所長，

名人簡介

Honoré de Balzac（巴爾扎克）(1799—1850)，詳見第 40 篇。

unindulgent criticisms.... And his deep sense of gratitude for what she had done never left him: "She has created my heart.... She is sixty, her sufferings have so changed her that you wouldn't know her, and my love has doubled." And long after her death he called after her, "... In times of great stress she supported me by her words, her deeds, and her devotion. If I am alive, it is thanks only to her. She was my moral sun."

— E. Ludwig[3]

3. E. Ludwig：路德維格，詳見第 4 篇的註釋。

給予他慎重的、毫不縱容的批評。……為此，巴爾扎克始終深懷對她感激之情，說：“她造就了我的心靈。……她已經六十歲，生活的磨難把她變得認不出來了，而我對她的愛卻有增無減。”在她去世很久以後，巴爾扎克追憶她說：“……在極為困難的時候，她以自己的言行和愛心給我支持。如果說我還健在的話，這完全多虧了她。她是我心靈的太陽。”

——〔德〕路德維格

43 Three Masters Skating Together

Henry Thoreau[1] is an experienced skater, and was skating dithyrambic dances.... Next to him followed Mr. Hawthorne, wrapped in his cloak, moved like a self-impelled Greek statue, stately and grave. Mr. Emerson[2] closed the line, evidently too weary to hold himself erect, pitching headforemost, half lying on the air.

— Mrs. Hawthorne[3]

---

1. Henry David Thoreau (1817 — 1862)：梭羅，美國作家，超驗主義（transcendentalism）運動的代表人物，代表作有《沃爾登或林中生活》(*Walden or Life in the Woods*, 1854)，其《論公民的不服從》(*Civil Disobedience*, 1849)一文影響巨大。
2. Ralph Waldo Emerson (1803—1882)：愛默生，美國思想家、散文作家、詩人，美國超驗主義運動的主要代表，著有《論自然》(*Nature*, 1836)、《詩集》(*Poems*, 1846)、《五月節》(*May-Day and Other Pieces*, 1867)等。
3. Mrs. Hawthorne：霍桑的妻子。

四十三　高手滑冰

亨利·梭羅是一位滑冰老手，此刻他正在展示充滿激情的舞姿。……尾隨其後的是霍桑先生，他身披斗篷，滑動起來像一尊能自己推動的希臘雕像，穩重而莊嚴。滑在最後的是愛默生先生。很明顯，由於他無精打彩，沒把身體挺直，而是把頭伸向前方，半個身子懸空平躺着。

——*〔美〕霍桑夫人*

名人簡介

Nathaniel Hawthorne（霍桑）(1804—1864)，美國小說家，其作品開創了美國象徵小說的傳統，代表作為長篇小說《紅字》(*The Scarlet Letter*, 1850)。

44 Anybody Can Do That

Tennyson's pipe was almost indispensable to him, and I remember one time when I and several friends were staying at his house, the question of tobacco turned up. Some of his friends taunted Tennyson that he could never give up tobacco. "Anybody can do that," he said, "if he chooses to do it." When his friends still continued to doubt and tease him, "Well," he said, "I shall give up smoking from tonight." The very same evening I was told that he threw his tobacco and pipe out the window of his bedroom. The next day he became very moody and captious, the third day no one knew what to do with him. But after a disturbed night I was told that he got out of bed in the morning, went quietly into the garden, picked up one of his pipes, stuffed it with the remains of the tobacco scattered about, and then having had a few puffs came to breakfast all right again.

— *M. Mueller*[1]

---

1. Max Mueller： 穆埃勒，丁尼生的朋友。

四十四　戒煙

煙斗對丁尼生來説幾乎是必不可少的。記得有一次，我和幾個朋友留住他家時，議論到吸煙的問題。他的朋友中有人譏笑他，説他永遠也戒不了煙。他説：“如果決意要做的話，任何人都做得到。”在朋友們繼續懷疑和戲弄他的時候，他便説：“我今晚就戒煙。”就在當天晚上，有人告訴我，他把煙絲和煙斗從他臥室的窗口扔了出去。第二天他變得鬱鬱寡歡，吹毛求疵。到了第三天，大家都拿他沒辦法了。可是，又一個不安的夜晚之後，我獲悉，他早晨起了牀便悄悄地走進花園，揀起一隻煙斗，把散落的剩餘煙絲裝進煙斗。他噴出幾團煙霧之後，便過來用早餐，情緒恢復如初。

——〔英〕*穆埃勒*

名人簡介

Alfred Tennyson（丁尼生）(1809—1892)，英國詩人，其詩音韻和諧，詞藻華麗，1850 年被封為桂冠詩人，主要詩作有《夏洛蒂小姐》(*The Lady of Shalott*, 1832)、《尤利西斯》(*Ulysses*, 1842)等。

45 Writing While Chatting

One night in Doughty Street, Mrs. Charles Dickens, my wife and myself were sitting round the fire cosily enjoying a chat, when Dickens, for some purpose came suddenly into the room. "What, you here!" he exclaimed; "I'll bring my work." It was his monthly portion of *Oliver Twist*[1] for Bentley's. In a few minutes he returned, manuscript in hand, and while he was pleasantly discoursing he employed himself in carrying to a corner of the room a little table, at which he seated himself and recommenced his writing. We, at his bidding, went on talking our "little nothings,"— he, every now and then (the feather of his pen still moving rapidly from side to side), put in a cheerful interlude. It was interesting to watch, upon the sly[2], the mind and the muscles working. And to note the working brow, the set of the mouth, with the tongue tightly pressed against the closed lips, as was his habit.

— *H. Burnett*[3]

1. *Oliver Twist*： 小說名，另有譯名為《苦海孤雛》。
2. (up)on the sly： 偷偷地，秘密地。
3. Henry Burnett： 伯內特，狄更斯的好友。

四十五　筆耕

在道蒂街的一個夜晚，我和查爾斯・狄更斯太太，還有我的夫人，舒適愜意地圍坐在火爐旁，欣然閒聊。突然間，狄更斯不知有什麼事來到房間裏。"怎麼，你們在這兒呀！"他驚喊道，"我去把我的活兒拿來。"這活兒是他為賓特萊的雜誌撰寫的每月一期的《奧列佛・退斯特》連載稿。幾分鐘後，他拿着手稿回來了。他一邊樂呵呵地説着話，一邊自己動手把一張小桌子挪到房間的一個角落裏，坐定了就動手寫起來。我們依照他的吩咐，繼續談着那些無關緊要的事情，而他(只見他筆上的羽毛迅速地從稿紙的一端移到另一端)時而還會高興地插上幾句。暗中看着他的腦和肌體正在工作，注意到他那正在思索的眉梢，舌頭用力頂着抿合的雙脣時的那種嘴形的習慣，真叫人覺得饒有趣味。

——〔英〕伯內特

名人簡介

Charles Dickens（狄更斯）(1812—1870)，英國作家，作品甚多，重要的有《匹克威克外傳》(*Pickwick Papers*, 1836—37)、《大衛・科波菲爾》(*David Copperfield*, 1849—50)、《雙城記》(*A Tale of Two Cities*, 1859)等。

46 The Most Precious Moment

When I was a very young man I had a mistress, a miller's wife from the outskirts of St. Petersburg, whom I used to see when out hunting. She was charming, pale as dawn with a cast in one eye, which is quite common among our people. She would take nothing from me. Then one day she said to me, "You must give me something." "What do you want?" "Bring me some soap." I brought her the soap. She took it and went away, then came back and blushing said to me, holding out her perfumed hands, "Kiss my hands like you kiss the hands of the ladies in the drawing rooms in St. Petersburg." I threw myself at her feet. I can tell you, there had been no moment of my life more precious than that one.

— I. S. Turgenev

四十六　最珍貴的一刻

在我還很年輕的時候，有過一個情婦。她是聖彼得堡郊外的一個磨坊主的妻子。我外出打獵時，常與她見面。她嫵媚動人，晨曦般的玉顏，一隻眼睛略微斜視，這在我們俄國人中是相當普遍的。她總不問我要東西。後來有一天，她對我説：“你一定要給我點東西。”“你要什麼呢？”“給我點肥皂吧。”我給她帶去了肥皂。她接了過去就走開了。過後她又回來了，伸出芳香的雙手，紅着臉對我説：“吻我的手，就像你在聖彼得堡的客廳裏吻那些貴婦人的手一樣。”我頓時拜倒在她的面前。我可以告訴你，在我的一生中還未曾有過比這更為珍貴的時刻。

——〔俄〕屠格涅夫

名人簡介

Ivan Sergeevich Turgenev（屠格涅夫）(1818—1883)：俄國作家，其作品對俄羅斯文學和世界文學都有很大影響，主要作品有特寫集《獵人筆記》(*A Sportsman's Sketches*, 1852)、劇本《村居一月》(*A Month in the Country*, 1855)、長篇小説《父與子》(*Fathers and Sons*, 1862) 等。

47 The Return to the Mississippi

In 1876 Mark Twain published *The Adventures of Tom Sawyer* and in the same year he began what he called "another boy's book."[1] ... He pigeonholed it long before it was done and for as much as four years. In 1880 he took it out and carried it forward a little, only to abandon it again. He had a theory of unconscious composition and believed that a book must write itself; ...

But then in the summer of 1882 Mark Twain was possessed by a charge of literary energy which, as he wrote to a friend, was more intense than any he had experienced for many years. He worked all day and every day, and periodically he so fatigued himself that he had to recruit his strength by a day or two of smoking and reading in bed. It is impossible not to suppose that this great creative drive was connected with — was perhaps the direct result of — the

1. another boy's book：指 *The Adventures of Huckleberry Finn*，1884 年出版。

四十七　舊地重遊

1876年馬克·吐溫出版了《湯姆·索耶歷險記》，於同年開始了他稱之為“另外一本孩子的書”的寫作。……書稿未成，他卻早就把它束之高閣。一停便是四年之久。1880年他拿出書稿，稍有進展，卻又擱置起來。他有一種理論，叫做無意識寫作，認為一本書的寫作必須是水到渠成的。……

但是，在1882年夏天的時候，馬克·吐溫迸發出一股寫作勁頭。正如他在給一位友人的信中所寫的那樣，這股勁比起許多年來他所體驗到的更為強烈。他整日工作，每天都是這樣，時常把自己累得不得不在牀上躺上一兩天，抽抽煙，看看書，以此來恢復體力。人們不能不想到，這股偉大的創作動力與那年早些時候他遊覽密西西比河有關

名人簡介

Mark Twain（馬克·吐溫）(1835—1910)，美國作家，當過排字工人、船上舵手和新聞記者，以語言幽默見長。他的作品很多，本篇描述他創作長篇小説《哈克貝里·費恩歷險記》的一些情況。該書成為世界名著，又一次説明生活是文學和藝術的源泉。這可比較第 64 篇有關達·芬奇作畫過程中不時回返大自然，及第 68 篇貝多芬創作離不開大自然等情節。

visit to the Mississippi he had made earlier in the year, the trip which forms the matter of the second part of *Life on the Mississippi*[2]. His boyhood and youth on the river he so profoundly loved had been at once the happiest and most significant part of Mark Twain's life; his return to it in middle age stirred vital memories which revived and refreshed the idea of *Huckleberry Finn*. Now at last the book was not only ready but eager to write itself. ...

... It is his masterpiece, and perhaps he learned to know that. But he could scarcely have estimated it for what it is, one of the world's great books and one of the central documents of American culture.

— *L. Trilling*[3]

---

2. *Life on the Mississippi*： 1883 年出版。
3. Lionel Trilling (1905—1975)： 特里林，美國文學評論家，著有《弗洛伊德和我們的文化危機》(*Freud and the Crisis of Our Culture*, 1955)、《文化之外》(*Beyond Culture*, 1965)、《真誠與真實性》(*Sincerity and Authenticity*, 1972)等。

聯，也許就是這次遊覽的直接效果。那次旅行成了《密西西比河上的生活》第二部分的素材。他如此鍾愛密西西比河，他的青少年時期都是在那裏度過的。這時期正是馬克．吐溫一生中最幸福、最有意義的部分。在他中年時期，馬克．吐溫重返密西西比河，舊地重遊激起了他重要的回憶。這使得《哈克貝里．費恩歷險記》的創作思想得以復甦，變得清晰了。這時，這本書不但終於成熟，而且已經到了落筆成章的時候了。……

……這是他的傑作，也許這一點他從別人那裏得知。但是，他萬萬不會評價這書為世界名著之一，是美國文化的重要文獻。

——〔美〕特里林

48 Books for Signature

He[1] was dining once with Thomas Hardy, and as they were finishing their coffee he asked Hardy the very same question. "What do you do, Hardy, about books that are sent to you for signature?"

"Yeats," said Hardy, "come with me, there is something upstairs I want to show you." At the top of the house Hardy opened a door, and the two poets entered a larger room. This room was covered from floor to ceiling with books. Hardy waved his hand at the odd-thousand volumes that filled the room. — "Yeats," said he, "these are the books that were sent to me for signature."

— *J. Stephens*[2]

---

1. He：指 William Butler Yeats (1865 — 1939)：葉芝，愛爾蘭詩人、劇作家，獲 1923 年諾貝爾文學獎，詩作有《鐘樓》 (*The Tower*, 1927)、《盤旋的樓梯》(*The Winding Stair*, 1929)等。
2. James Stephens (1880 — 1950)：斯蒂芬斯，愛爾蘭作家、詩人，著有小説《金罐子》(*The Crock of Gold*, 1912)、《女傭的女兒》(*The Charwoman's Daughter*, 1912)、詩集《叛亂》(*Insurrections*, 1909)等。

四十八　為書簽名

有一次，他和托馬斯·哈代一起吃飯。就要喝完咖啡時，他向哈代提了那個老問題："哈代，那些寄來要你簽名的書，你怎麼處理？"

"葉芝，"哈代說，"跟我來，我樓上有東西要給你看。"在頂樓上哈代打開了一扇房門。兩位詩人走進一間較大的房間。房間裏的書從地板一直堆到了天花板。朝着這一房間的千多冊書，哈代揮揮手說："葉芝，這些就是寄來要我簽名的書。"

——〔英〕斯蒂芬斯

名人簡介

Thomas Hardy（哈代）(1840—1928)，英國小說家、詩人，代表作為小說《德伯家的苔絲》(*Tess of the d'Urbervilles*, 1891)、《無名的裘德》(*Jude the Obscure*, 1895)、歷史詩劇《列王》(*Dynasts*, 1903—08)等。

49 The Book Made a Difference

Thomas Hardy asked me to lunch, and I bicycled over from our cottage at Studland. There were only he and I and his wife — the first Mrs. Hardy, of course — at the meal; it was about the time when *Jude the Obscure*[1] had been published, and I was loud in my praise of that work. Mrs. Hardy was far from sharing my enthusiasm. It was the first novel of his, she told me, that he had published without first letting her read the manuscript: had she read it, she added firmly, it would not have been published, or at least, not without considerable emendations. The book had made a difference to them, she added, in the County. ...

The position was awkward for me, and very embarrassing. Hardy said nothing, and did not lift his eyes from the plate; I was hard put to it to manufacture some kind of conversation, and it was a great relief when Mrs. Hardy rose, and left us.... Even then Hardy's silence persisted, till I

---

1. *Jude the Obscure*：此小說於 1895年發表，遭到眾多責難，認為作者在宗教和道德觀上極為墮落。

四十九　招致非議

托馬斯·哈代邀我吃午飯。我從位於斯圖蘭的住所騎自行車前往。用餐時就只有他和我，還有他的妻子——當然是第一位哈代夫人。當時差不多正是他的小說《無名的裘德》剛出版的時候。我為這部著作大加讚揚。哈代夫人卻與我的那種熱情大相徑庭。她告訴我，哈代發表小說未經她預先閱讀手稿的這是第一部。她用堅定的口吻接着說，要是她讀過的話，這部小說就不會出版。至少也要經過重大校訂之後才能得以出版。她還說，這本書使郡裏的人對他們夫婦倆開始另有看法。……

這種狀況使我很尷尬，不知所措。哈代一聲不吭，只顧埋頭用他那份盤中餐。我怎麼也想不出個話題來交談。當哈代夫人起身離開時，我們如釋重負……。即使在這個

名人簡介

Thomas Hardy（哈代）(1840—1928)，詳見第 48 篇。

told him of a bird in our wood whose identity puzzled us; we had discovered at last that it was a corncrake. Hardy brightened at once, the cloud lighted, and we talked, talked of birds and trees, evidently a favourite subject of his, till I left.

— *A. Sutro*[2]

2. Alfred Sutro (1863—1933)：薩特羅，英國劇作家。

時候，哈代仍舊默不作聲，直到我告訴他，我的林子裏有隻鳥，我怎麼也弄不清這鳥的屬類，這時他才和我談起來。最後我們認定這隻鳥是一隻秧雞。哈代立刻興奮起來，陰雲散去。我們談鳥，談樹，無疑，這些是他最感興趣的話題。談話一直持續到我告辭。

——〔英〕薩特羅

50 He Lived for Talking

That was what he lived for, talking, writing that was also loud talk in ink, and editing. He was a brilliant editor for a time and then the impetus gave out and he flagged rapidly. So soon as he ceased to work vehemently he became unable to work. He could not attend to things without excitement. As his confidence went he became clumsily loud.

His talk was most effective at the first hearing; after some experience of it, it began to bore me so excessively that I avoided the office when I knew he was there. There was no variety in his posing and no fancy in his falsehoods. I do not remember that he said a single good thing in all that uproar; ... Always he was proclaiming himself the journalistic Robin Hood[1], bold yet strangely sensitive and tender-hearted — with the full volume of his voice. The reader may get the quality of it best in his book *The Man Shakespeare*.

— *H. G. Wells*[2]

---

1. Robin Hood：羅賓漢，英國民間傳說中劫富濟貧的綠林好漢。
2. Herbert George Wells：威爾斯，詳見第 51 篇。

五十　高談闊論

他活着就是為了談論、寫作（用筆墨進行也屬大聲談論）和編輯。他曾經一度是個才華橫溢的編輯，以後他的工作熱情消失殆盡，很快便一蹶不振。他停止狂熱地工作後不久，乾脆就不能工作了。他不能做一些毫無興趣的事情。隨着自信心的消失，他説話變得大聲聒耳。

他的談話初聽起來效果最好。聽過他一些談論之後，我開始感到極其枯燥乏味，以致只要我知道他在辦公室裏，就不去那兒了。他説話的姿勢一成不變，虛言妄語中沒有一點想像力。我不記得他在所有這些吵嚷聲中説過一件有意義的事。……他總是標榜自己是新聞業的羅賓漢，有着一副響亮的嗓門，敢做敢為，卻又是奇特地多愁善感，菩薩心腸。讀者可以從他寫的《莎翁其人》一書中充分領略到這種特點。

——〔英〕威爾斯

名人簡介

Frank Harris (哈里斯)(1856 — 1931)，英國新聞記者、作家，曾僑居美國，在英國主編過《星期六評論》(*Saturday Review*) 等刊物，寫過莎士比亞、王爾德等人的傳記，以自傳 *My Life and Loves* (1923) 聞名，因書中自我揭露性方面的內容而遭抨擊。

51 A Duologue[1]

Then it was that my Destiny saw fit to bring a grave little figure into my life who was to be its ruling influence and support throughout all my most active years. When I came into my laboratory to meet the new students who were assembling for the afternoon class of 1892-93 I found two exceptionally charming young women making friends at the end table. ...

If either of these young ladies had joined my class alone I should probably never have become very intimate with either.... But with two students capable of asking intelligent questions it was the most natural thing in the world to put a stool between them, sit down instructively, and let these questions expand. They were both in a phase of mental formation and student curiosity, they were both reading widely,... Catherine Robbins had read more widely and had a bolder curiosity.... The snatches of talk for four or five

1. 本篇選自 H.G. Wells 所著 *Experiment in Autobiography* (1934) 一書，描述他執教生物課時與一女學生羅賓斯建立了友誼，彼此成為對方的知音。不久，羅賓斯成了威爾斯夫人。

五十一　心連心

那麼，這是命中注定，一個重要的小人兒走進我的生活。她在我整個年富力強的歲月中給予我舉足輕重的影響和支持。我走進實驗室，與1892—93學年的新生見面，他們是來上午後課的。這時，我看到兩名相貌出眾的女青年坐在最後的一張桌子旁，在那裏作新友交談。……

如果兩人中只有一個單獨來聽我講課，我就不會與其中的任何一個建立親密的關係了。……可是由於這兩個學生能夠提出一些聰明的問題，我搬個凳子放在她們中間，坐下來解答問題，再把這些問題展開，這樣做是很自然的事情。她們倆正處於智力發展、求知慾強的階段。兩個人都在廣泛閱讀，……凱瑟琳．羅賓斯讀書的範圍更廣一些，求知慾也更強。……課上不時地進行的、每次連續四

名人簡介

Herbert George Wells（威爾斯）(1866—1946)，英國作家，著有科幻小說《時間機器》(*The Time Machine*, 1895)、《隱身人》(*The Invisible Man*, 1897)、《星際戰爭》(*The War of the Worlds*, 1898)等；社會問題小說《基普斯》(*Kipps*, 1905)、《托諾．邦蓋》(*Tono-Bungay*, 1909)等；以及歷史著作《世界史綱》(*The Outline of History*, 1920)等。威爾斯的第一次婚姻並不幸福，兩人之間的差異導致離婚。

minutes at a stretch that were possible during the class session were presently not enough for us, and we developed a habit of meeting early and going on talking after the two hours of rigorous biology were over. Little Miss Robbins was the more acutely interested and she was generally more punctually in advance of her time than her friend, so that we two became a duologue masked as a three-cornered friendship.

— H. G. Wells

五分鐘的交談對我們來說已經不夠了。於是我們養成了一個習慣，上課前早些見面，而且在兩個小時嚴謹的生物課結束後再繼續談下去。嬌小的羅賓斯小姐顯出更強烈的興趣。一般來說，她總是比她的朋友更準時提前到來。就這樣，我們的談話在三人友誼的幌子下變成了兩個人之間的對話了。

——〔英〕威爾斯

52 Ever Thought of Suicide?

Untypically for Wells the conversation tailed off. The silences got longer and longer. Without any introduction, he broke into the quiet. It was a simple question. He said, "Ever thought of suicide[1], Snow?" I reflected. I said, "Yes, Herbert George, I have." He replied, "So have I. But not till I was past seventy." He was then seventy-two. We drank some more whisky and looked sombrely at the palms. (They were sitting in a hotel lounge, under the potted palms, after midnight.)

— *C. P. Snow*[2]

---

1. suicide：威爾斯一生為爭取實現一個無戰爭、無不合理現象的理想社會而奮鬥，然而未見實現，不免悲觀失望。這可見於他逝世前一年寫的最後一篇作品《到達極限的理智》(*Mind at the End of Its Tether*, 1945)。文中他總結了自己對生活的思考和看法。
2. Charles Percy Snow (1905—1980)：斯諾，英國小說家、物理學家和外交家，主要著作有包括十一卷的系列小說《陌生人和弟兄們》(*Strangers and Brothers*, 1940—70)、論文《兩種文化與科學革命》(*The Two Cultures and the Scientific Revolution*, 1959)等。

五十二　想過自殺？

我們的談話漸漸地變得無話可說了，威爾斯這樣的表現是異常的。一次次的沉默拖得越來越長。突然，他沒先說些什麼，便打破沉默。那是個很直率的問題。他問：“斯諾，你想過自殺嗎？”我想了想，說：“是的，赫伯特·喬治，我想過。”他接着說：“我也想過。不過，我七十多歲才想的。”他那時七十二歲。我們又喝了些威士忌酒，悶悶不樂地望着棕櫚樹。(當時已過午夜，他們坐在酒店大廳的盆栽棕櫚樹下。)

——〔英〕斯諾

名人簡介

Herbert George Wells (威爾斯)(1866—1946)，詳見第 51 篇。

53 Burgess Coined "Blurb"

It is the custom of [American] publishers to present copies of a conspicuous current book to booksellers attending the annual dinner of their trade association, and as this little book[1] was in its heyday when the meeting took place I gave it to 500 guests. These copies were differentiated from the regular edition by the addition of a comic bookplate drawn by the author and by a special jacket which he devised. It was the common practice to print the picture of a damsel ... on the jacket of every novel, so Burgess lifted from a Lydia Pinkham[2] or tooth-powder advertisement the portrait of a sickly sweet young woman, painted in some gleaming teeth, and otherwise enhanced her pulchritude, and placed her in the center of the jacket. His accompanying text was some nonsense about "Miss Belinda Blurb," and thus the term supplied a real need and became a fixture in our language.

— *B. W. Huebsch*[3]

---

1. this little book：指 Burgess 所著 *Are You a Bromide?* (1907)。
2. Lydia Pinkham (1819 — 1883)：平凱姆，美國專賣藥製造商，她的姓名成為藥品的名稱，其藥品的廣告在美國流傳廣泛。
3. B. W. Huebsch：休士，為 Burgess 出版著作的出版商。

五十三　伯吉斯造詞

〔美國〕出版商在他們商會的周年晚宴上向到會的各位書商贈送一些當時出色的暢銷書，這已成慣例。酒會期間，這本篇幅不大的書正處於最熱銷的時期，所以我把它贈送給與會的五百位賓客。這些贈書不同於一般版本，而是附加了作者畫的逗人的藏書籤和作者設計的護封。當時的通常做法是在每一本小說的護封上印上一個青年女子的畫像……於是，伯吉斯借用平凱姆或是牙粉廣告，把一個病態美的青年女子的肖像印在護封的中央，再畫上一些光潔的牙齒，或者突出其俏麗的容貌。附在旁邊的一段文字是他胡編亂造的關於"比琳達·勃樂布小姐"的一些話。就是這樣，"勃樂布"（blurb）這個詞不僅滿足了實際需要，而且成為我們語言中的一個固定的單詞了。

——〔美〕休士

名人簡介

F. Gelett Burgess（伯吉斯）(1866—1951)，美國幽默作家和插圖畫家，曾任幽默雜誌《雲雀》編輯，著有自作插圖的《野孩子和野孩子的形成》(*Goops and How to Be Them*, 1900)等。他創造了 blurb 一詞（詞意是：印在書籍等護封上的簡介或推薦廣告）。

54 A Lost Generation

She had some ignition trouble with the old Model T Ford she then drove and the young man who worked in the garage and had served in the last year of the war had not been adept, or perhaps had not broken the priority of other vehicles, in repairing Miss Stein's Ford. Anyway, he had not been *sérieux*[1] and had been corrected severely by the patron of the garage after Miss Stein's protest. The patron had said to him, "You are all a *génération perdue*[2]."

"That's what you are. That's what you all are," Miss Stein said. "All of you young people who served in the war. You are a lost generation."

— *Hemingway*[3]

---

1. *sérieux*：〔法語〕serious。
2. *génération perdue*：〔法語〕lost generation。
3. Ernest Hemingway (1899 — 1961)：海明威，美國小說家，早期為"迷惘的一代"的代表人物。獲1954年諾貝爾文學獎，代表作有《太陽照樣升起》(*The Sun Also Rises*, 1926)、《永別了，武器》(*A Farewell to Arms*, 1929)、《戰地鐘聲》(*For Whom the Bell Tolls*, 1940)等。此篇描述了名句"迷惘的一代"(the lost generation)的來源之一。

五十四　迷惘的一代

她當時用的那輛福特T型舊車點火發動時有些毛病。在汽車修理廠工作的年青人曾在戰爭的最後一個年頭裏在軍隊服役過。他的修理技術本來就不行，或許在為斯泰因小姐的福特車修理中，他未能給予破例服務，而仍舊優先照顧了其他車輛。不管怎麼說，他就是沒有認真對待此事。斯泰因小姐提出抗議後，這個工人受到了修理廠老闆的嚴厲責備："你們全都是迷惘的一代。"

"你就是那樣的人，你們全都是那樣的人，"斯泰因說："你們這些在戰爭中服役過的年青人都是。你們是迷惘的一代。"

——〔美〕海明威

名人簡介

Gertrude Stein（斯泰因）(1874—1946)，美國女作家，提倡先鋒派藝術(avant-gardism)。1903年起僑居巴黎，她的家成為當時名流作家和藝術家的沙龍，作品有《三個女人的一生》(*Three Lives*, 1908)、《艾麗斯．B．托克拉斯自傳》(*The Autobiography of Alice B. Toklas*, 1933)等。

55 Extremely Capricious

Willie[1] can be extremely capricious. He can turn violently against an old friend for some quite small reason.... One day recently Willie was walking in the garden with his companion, Alan Searle, when they stopped in their tracks[2] to watch the progress of a snail. Alan picked up a small bit of gravel and tossed it at the snail. Willie shouted: "Don't do that!" Alan threw another little pebble. The next thing Alan knew: he was lying with an unrecognizable face in a nearby hospital.

— *C. Beaton*[3]

---

1. Willie：William 的暱稱，指 William Somerset Maugham（毛姆）。
2. in their tracks：where they stand，即就地，當場。
3. Cecil Beaton (1904 — 1980)：比頓，英國攝影師、舞台服裝設計師。

五十五　非常任性

威利有時非常任性。他會由於很小的原因而對老朋友氣勢洶洶地翻臉。……不久前的一天，威利與同伴阿蘭·瑟爾一起在花園裏漫步。突然，他們停下來觀看一隻蝸牛蠕蠕而動。阿蘭拾起一塊礫石，朝蝸牛扔去。威利喊道：“別扔！”阿蘭卻又扔了一塊小石子。接下來他知道的事情是自己已經躺在附近一家醫院裏，臉被打得認不出來了。

——〔英〕比頓

名人簡介

William Somerset Maugham（毛姆）(1874—1965)，英國小説家、戲劇家，作品基調憤世嫉俗，著有長篇小説《人間的枷鎖》(*Of Human Bondage*, 1915)、劇本《社交界》(*The Circle*, 1921)等。

56 A Merchant Prince

I was born in the working-class. Early I discovered enthusiasm, ambition, and ideals: and to satisfy these became the problem of my child-life. ...

...

..., and I had a vision of myself becoming a baldheaded and successful merchant prince.

Alas for vision! When I was sixteen I had already earned the title of "prince." But this title was given me by a gang of cut-throats and thieves, by whom I was called "The Prince of the Oyster Pirates." ... I owned a boat and a complete oyster-pirating outfit. ...

... One night I went on a raid amongst the Chinese fishermen.... It was robbery, I grant, but it was precisely the spirit of capitalism. The capitalist takes away the possessions of his fellow-creatures by means of a rebate, or of a betrayal of trust, or by the purchase of senators and supreme-court judges. I was merely crude. That was the only difference. I used a gun.

— Jack London

五十六　富商

我出身勞工階層。我很早就滿懷熱忱，有抱負，有理想。實現抱負和理想就成了我孩提生活中的一個問題。……

……

……，我幻想自己成為一個成功的禿頭富商。

哎呀，夢想而已！十六歲時，我就已經獲得“大王”的頭銜。但是這頭銜是一幫歹徒和小偷們給我起的。他們叫我“牡蠣海盜王子”。……我有一艘小船和一整套搶劫牡蠣的工具。……

……一個晚上，我和中國漁民一起去搶掠。……我承認，那是一次搶劫，但恰好是資本主義精神。資本家就是通過剋扣、背信棄義或買通議員和最高法院的大法官的手段，奪走同胞的財產。我只不過不加掩飾，這就是唯一不同的地方。我用了槍。

——〔美〕傑克．倫敦

名人簡介

Jack London（傑克．倫敦）(1876—1916)，美國作家，出身下層，飽嚐顛沛流離之苦。作品以浪漫主義手法描寫爭取生存的原始鬥爭，有自傳體小說《馬丁．伊登》(*Martin Eden*, 1909) 及小說《荒野的呼喚》(*The Call of the Wild*, 1903)、《鐵蹄》(*The Iron Heel*, 1907)等。本篇描述他為了擺脱貧困與人合夥搶劫海邊牡蠣養殖場。

57 I Became a Tramp

... I was not afraid of work. I loved hard work.

...as luck would have it, I found an employer.... I thought I was learning a trade. In reality, I had displaced two men. I thought he was making an electrician out of me; as a matter of fact, he was making fifty dollars per month out of me. The two men I had displaced had received forty dollars each per month; I was doing the work of both for thirty dollars per month.

This employer worked me nearly to death.... Too much work sickened me. I did not wish ever to see work again. I fled from work. I became a tramp, begging my way from door to door, wandering over the United States and sweating bloody sweats in slums and prisons.

— Jack London

五十七 流浪漢

……我不怕幹活，我喜歡幹艱苦的活兒。

……我還算走運，找到了一位僱主。……我以為我要學一門手藝了。事實上我頂替了兩個人幹的活。我想，他要培養我成為一名電工。而實際上，他每月從我身上賺取五十美元。我頂替的那兩個人的工資是每人每月四十美元。我幹的是兩個人的活，每月只得三十美元。

這個僱主讓我幹得差點累死。……過於沉重的工作使我厭煩。我不想再碰上工作了。我逃走不幹了，成了流浪漢，挨戶乞討，浪跡整個美國。血腥的汗水流淌在貧民窟和監獄裏。

—〔美〕傑克．倫敦

名人簡介

Jack London（傑克．倫敦）(1876－1916)，詳見第 56 篇。

58 He Walked in My Door

At once I found that writing was fun. I even forgot I hadn't seen Sherwood Anderson for three weeks until he walked in my door, the first time he ever came to see me, and said "What's wrong? Are you mad at me?" I told him I was writing a book. He said, "My God," and walked out. When I finished the book — it was *Soldier's Pay*[1] — I met Mrs. Anderson on the street. She asked how the book was coming, and I said I'd finished it. She said, "Sherwood says that he will make a trade with you. If he doesn't have to read your manuscript he will tell his publisher to accept it." I said, "Done," and that's how I became a writer.

— *W. Faulkner*[2]

---

1. *Soldier's Pay*：W. Faulkner 寫的第一部小說，1926 年出版.
2. William Faulkner (1897—1962)：福克納，美國小說家，美國"南方文學"流派的代表人物，1949年獲諾貝爾文學獎，代表作有《聲音與憤怒》(*The Sound and the Fury*, 1929)、《秋光》(*Light in August*, 1932)等。

五十八　登門拜訪

我很快發現寫作很有趣。我甚至忘了已有三個星期沒有見到舍伍德·安德森了，直到他來登門拜訪。這是他平素第一次來看我。他說："怎麼啦？生我的氣啦？"我告訴他我正在寫一本書。他說了句"天哪"就離去了。這本書——《軍餉》——寫完之後，我在大街上見到了安德森太太。她問起這本書的進展情況，我回答已經完稿了。她說："舍伍德說了要與你做一筆交易。如果他無須讀你的手稿的話，他就讓他的出版商接受你的書。"我說："行啊！"我就是這樣成為一名作家的。

——〔美〕福克納

名人簡介

Sherwood Anderson（安德森）(1876—1941)，美國作家，美國文學中現代文體風格的開創人之一，代表作有短篇小說集《俄亥俄州瓦恩斯堡鎮》(*Winesburg, Ohio*, 1919)等。

59 I Cannot Go On

I have a feeling I shall go mad. I cannot go on longer in these terrible times. I hear voices and cannot concentrate on my work. I have fought against it but cannot fight any longer. I owe all my happiness to you but cannot go on and spoil your life.

— *Virginia Woolf*

五十九　活不下去

我有一種感覺，要瘋了。在這些十分難受的時刻，我再也不能活下去了。耳際是人們的說話聲，我不能專心工作。我抗爭，可是再也掙扎不下去了。虧得你，才有我的一切幸福，可是我不能繼續活下去，擾亂你的生活了。

——〔英〕吳爾夫

名人簡介

Virginia Woolf(吳爾夫)(1882—1941)，英國女小說家、評論家，運用內心獨白和意識流手法寫作，著有長篇小說《海浪》(*The Waves*, 1931)、《黛洛維夫人》(*Mrs. Dalloway*, 1925)等。她於 1912 年與作家 Leonard Woolf 結婚。這裏的選段是她因受不了病痛折磨而溺水自殺前，給她丈夫的留言。

60 Taste in Music

In regard to music he is oddly fastidious. He possesses a magnificent tenor voice....

His fastidious taste in music leads him to throw his arms wide open to the future. Last year Mlle[1] Monnier ... gathered some cultural musicians together one evening to hear the latest thing in modern music by an American composer, Anthil or Antheil[2]. After a quarter of an hour of it many of the guests rose and went away, protesting and shouting. But Joyce declared, "He reminds me of Mozart[3]." I cannot doubt Joyce's sincerity.

— *E. Schmitz*[4]

---

1. Mlle：〔法語〕Mademoiselle (小姐) 的縮略語。
2. George Antheil (1900—1959)：安西爾，原名 Georg Johann Carl，美國作曲家，以極時髦的作品著稱。
3. Wolfgang Amadeus Mozart (1756 — 1791)：莫扎特，奧地利作曲家。
4. Ettore Schmitz (1861 — 1928)：施密茲，意大利小說家，喬伊斯旅居意大利時，曾當過他的英語家庭教師，還幫助他發表作品。

六十　音樂鑑賞力

在音樂方面，他出奇地講究。他具有優美的男高音歌喉。……

對音樂極高的鑑賞力使他樂於接受未來事物。去年的一個晚上莫尼埃小姐……會集了一些很有素養的音樂家，一起來聽美國作曲家安西爾創作的現代音樂最新作品。十五分鐘後，許多來賓提出抗議，大聲嚷着起身離去。然而，喬伊斯卻聲稱“他使我想起了莫扎特。”我不懷疑喬伊斯此話的真誠。

——〔意〕施密茲

名人簡介

James Joyce(喬伊斯)(1882—1941)，愛爾蘭小説家，作品揭露西方現代社會的腐朽一面，多用“意識流”(stream of consciousness)手法，代表作有長篇小説《尤利西斯》(*Ulysses*, 1922)、《菲尼根的甦醒》(*Finnegan's Wake*, 1939)等。

61 She Had Nothing to Read

Mrs. Joyce[1], a simple candid Irish woman, is very patient with her nervous husband, but she has little appreciation of his work. ...

In their living room not long ago, Mrs. Joyce remarked without the slightest ironical intent that she had nothing to read and wished she could get the works of some of the "good Irish humorists". Joyce glanced at me slyly and smiled. It is no secret that his wife has not read the major part of his writings. ...

Once, I know, he went to bed for two days because a man for whom he had not the slightest artistic regard wrote disparagingly of his recent efforts. When a mutual friend told him that James Stephens[2] had found his *Anna Livia Plurabelle* musical, Joyce's face lighted with joy which diminished only slightly when the friend added that Stephens had also said that he was sure the general public would never understand it.

— *E. Paul*[3]

---

1. Mrs. Joyce：她的丈夫是喬伊斯（James Joyce）。
2. James Stephens：斯蒂芬斯，詳見第 48 篇的註釋。
3. Elliot Harold Paul (1891—1958)：保羅，美國作家，著有長篇小說《一個西班牙城鎮的生與死》(*The Life and Death of a Spanish Town*, 1937)等。

六十一　沒書可讀

喬伊斯太太，一位樸實坦誠的愛爾蘭婦女，對她那位神經質的丈夫十分耐心，但對丈夫的寫作工作卻不大欣賞。……

不久前，在他們的起居室裏，喬伊斯太太說她沒有什麼書可讀。她說這話絲毫沒有諷刺的意思。她希望能弄到愛爾蘭出色的幽默作家的作品。喬伊斯偷偷地瞥了我一眼笑了。他的多半作品，他妻子還沒讀過。這不是什麼祕密。……

據我所知，他曾經一連睡了兩天，因為有一個他認為其藝術水平根本不屑一顧的人，對他近期的寫作竟表示輕蔑。一位我們共同的朋友告訴他，詹姆斯．斯蒂芬斯認為他寫的《安娜．利維亞．普魯拉貝爾》像音樂般悅耳。這時，他喜形於色。這位朋友又說，斯蒂芬斯確信，一般讀者不會理解這部作品。這時，喬伊斯的表情才稍有收斂。

——〔美〕保羅

名人簡介

James Joyce（喬伊斯）(1882－1941)，詳見第60篇。

62 Table Manners

Once, when I was quite little, he came up to the nursery while I was having my lunch. And while he was talking I paused between mouthfuls, resting my hands on the table, knife and fork pointing upwards. "You oughtn't really to sit like that," he said, gently. "Why not?" I asked, surprised. "Well...," he hunted around for a reason he could give. Because it's considered bad manners? Because you mustn't? Because... "Well," he said, looking in the direction that my fork was pointing, "suppose somebody suddenly fell through the ceiling. They might land on your fork and that would be very painful." "I see," I said, though I didn't really.

— *C. Milne*[1]

---

1. Christopher Milne：A · A · 米爾恩的兒子。

六十二　飯桌上的規矩

在我還很幼小的時候，他有一次到我托兒所裏來。當時我正在吃午飯。在他說話的時候，我每吃一口就停一停，還把兩隻手擱在桌上，手裏握着的刀叉朝上指着。他和聲細語地說：“你實在不該坐成這個樣子。”我感到驚訝，便問，“為什麼不能這樣坐？”“這個……”他極力想找出一個他能說出來的理由。因為大家認為這是一種不禮貌的舉止？因為你不應該這樣做？因為……“哦，”他邊說邊朝着我叉子指的方向看去。“假定有人突然從天花板上掉下來，他們可能會掉在你的叉子上，這會是很痛的呀！”我說：“我懂了。”儘管我事實上並不明白。

——〔英〕米爾恩

名人簡介

Alan Alexander Milne（米爾恩）(1882—1956)，英國詩人和劇作家，他寫的兒童讀物尤其受到歡迎，作品有輕喜劇《皮姆先生過去了》(*Mr. Pim Passes By*, 1919)、兒童故事《小熊溫尼普》(*Winnie-the-Pooh*, 1926)等。

Artists & Musicians
藝術家與音樂家

63 Observation

To paint a character from the Bible, for an old man, a beggar, or a shepherd, he would go to the public squares and the drinking dens, where he would be most likely to meet such persons. And he would draw a type or an animal from observation a hundred times before turning to his picture to fix it there for all time. He is said to have brought home peasants from the market and got them drunk in order to draw them. At the same time he was looking for laws; while studying the facial traits, he recorded the transitions in the closing and opening of the eyelid, the wrinkling of the nose, the pouting of the lips, in laughing, sneezing, yawning, cramps, perspiration, weariness, hunger — always he looked for the cause behind the expression which he was painting.

— E. Ludwig[1]

1. E. Ludwig：路德維格，詳見第 4 篇的註釋。

六十三　觀察

為了畫好取自《聖經》的人物，老人、乞丐，或者是牧羊人，達·芬奇總跑到那些公共廣場和酒吧去。他在那裏大概可以遇見這類人物。他總是把觀察到的人物或動物畫個上百次，才永久地固定在畫布上。據說他為了畫農民，曾把集市上的農民帶到家裏，讓他們喝得醉醺醺的，再作畫。同時，達·芬奇也在尋找規律。他在研究面部特徵時，便記錄眼瞼開合、鼻子折皺、噘嘴、大笑、打噴嚏、打呵欠、痙攣、流汗、疲倦、飢餓等時候的過渡變化——達·芬奇總是在探究被他描畫的表情背後的原因。

——〔德〕路德維格

名人簡介

Leonardo da Vinci（達·芬奇）(1452—1519)，意大利文藝復興時期畫家、雕塑家、建築師和工程師，在藝術和科學方面都有成就，代表作有壁畫《最後晚餐》(*Last Supper*, 1495—97)、肖像畫《蒙娜·麗莎》(*Mona Lisa*, 1503—06)等，著有《繪畫論》(*Treatise on Painting*, 1651)。

64 Vanished Suddenly

His life was a dialogue with nature.

...

... when he painted, he must be able to abandon the oil picture suddenly whenever he felt a change of mood and the desire to study some aspect of nature elsewhere.... Once — by the report of a Milanese, who saw him busy on the "Last Supper" — he painted the whole day, beginning at sunrise and standing on his scaffold without food or drink. Then again, he would not appear for days, or he would sit before the canvas for a couple of hours, silent and meditative, and then would leave again. Or he came into the church at midday after a ride on horseback, heated and excited, touched one of the figures with two strokes of his brush, and vanished.

— E. Ludwig[1]

1. E. Ludwig：路德維格，詳見第 4 篇的註釋。

六十四　説走就走

他的生活就是和大自然對話。

……

……他作畫的時候，不論何時，只要覺得心情有變化，想研究別處大自然的某個方面，他能突然丟下手頭的油畫。……一次，據看到他正在忙於畫《最後晚餐》的一個米蘭人講，達·芬奇有時會畫上整整一天。他從日出起就站在畫壁畫的支架上，不吃也不喝。隨後，又失蹤好幾天。或是在畫布前坐上好幾個小時，沉思不語，然後又離開。或者他在正午騎完馬之後，又熱又興奮地跑到教堂來，用畫筆在某個人物上畫上幾筆，接着，又不見蹤影。

——〔德〕路德維格

名人簡介

Leonardo da Vinci（達·芬奇）(1452－1519)，詳見第 63 篇。

65 A Human Story

In all history, there is but one artist who combines all the elements of self-portraiture: he alone depicts the various stages of a man's evolution. His self-portraits silently display a life: the yearning, despair, success, and tragedy of Rembrandt van Rijn. Rembrandt's life is so accurately disclosed in his series of self-portraits that one can find here a record of all his suffering and his elation.

Eighty-four self-portraits are now considered genuine, and fifty-eight of these are paintings. He painted the first when he was twenty-one, the last when he was sixty-three. During the intervening forty-two years exactly twice as many copies of himself were produced.

In his first picture, a young man examines the world with astute eyes — but the senses are sleeping. In the last, when the senses are again asleep, his eyes are turned inwardly.... There is more of a human story in this series of pictures than will be found in Rembrandt's actual biography.

— *E. Ludwig*[1]

---

1. E. Ludwig：路德維格，詳見第 4 篇的註釋。

六十五　人生歷程

縱觀歷史，只有一位藝術家，他匯總了自畫像的各個部分，即獨自描繪了一個人成長的各個階段。他的自畫像無聲地向人們展示了一個人的一生，即倫勃朗的憧憬、絕望、成功和悲劇。在倫勃朗的自畫像系列中，他的一生被如此準確地展示出來，人們能從中尋到畫家經歷的痛苦和歡樂的記錄。

有八十四幅自畫像現在被認作是真跡。其中五十八幅是油畫。他的第一幅畫作於二十一歲那年。最後一幅是六十三歲時完成的。其間的四十二年時間裏，他創作的自畫像恰好是這些年的兩倍。

他的第一幅作品中，一個年輕人用機敏的眼光審視着世界，不過他的理性還在沉睡。而最後這一幅，當理性再次沉睡的時候，畫中人的目光投向自己內心深處。……從這一系列繪畫作品中人們能瞭解到的有關畫家的人生經歷，要比讀他的傳記瞭解得更翔實。

——〔德〕路德維格

名人簡介

Rembrandt van Rijn（倫勃朗）(1606—1669)，荷蘭畫家、蝕刻家，擅長運用明暗對比，尤善於表現人物的神情和性格特徵，作品很多，如群像油畫《夜巡》(*The Nightwatch*, 1642)、蝕版畫《浪子回家》(*The Return of the Prodigal Son*, 1636)等。

66 Broken English

During this time[1], [Handel] applied to know whether there were any choirmen in the cathedral who could sing *at sight*: as he wished to prove some books that had been hastily transcribed, by trying the choruses which he intended to perform in Ireland.... Among them [was] a printer of the name of Janson, who had a good bass voice.... A time was fixed for this private rehearsal... but alas! on trial of the chorus in the *Messiah*, "And with his stripes we are healed," poor Janson, after repeated attempts failed so egregiously, that Handel, ...after swearing in four or five languages, cried out in broken English, "You shcauntrell, tit you not dell me dat you could sing at soit?"[2] "Yes, sir," [said] the printer, "and so I can, but not *at first sight*."

— *C. Burney*[3]

---

1. During this time：那時 Handel 在英國為首次上演其作品《彌賽亞》(*The Messiah*,1742) 做準備工作。
2. "You shcauntrell, ... soit?"：此句正確的讀法是："You scoundrel, did you not tell me that...at sight?"。
3. Charles Burney (1726—1814)：伯尼，英國作曲家。

六十六　蹩腳英文

在此期間，〔韓德爾〕提出想知道大教堂的唱詩班男歌手裏有沒有誰能就着歌譜作即席演唱，因為他想通過試唱那些預備在愛爾蘭演出時用的合唱曲目來核對一下匆忙編寫的樂譜。…… 在這些找來試唱的歌手中有位名叫詹森的印刷工。他天生一副很棒的男低音嗓子。…… 於是約定了這次私下排練的時間。…… 可是，唉！在試唱《彌賽亞》合唱曲〈因他受的鞭傷，我們得醫治〉的時候，可憐的詹森連唱幾次都極之失敗。韓德爾……一連用了四五種語言大罵之後，又操起蹩腳的英語大聲嚷道："你這個混蛋，你不是對我說過你會看譜就唱嗎？"印刷工說："是的，先生。我確實會看譜唱的，只是不會一看譜馬上就唱。"

——〔英〕伯尼

名人簡介

George Frederick Handel（韓德爾）(1685—1759)，英籍德國作曲家，創作甚多，包括歌劇、清唱劇、聲樂曲、樂器曲等，代表作有神劇《彌賽亞》(*The Messiah*)、管絃樂曲《水上音樂》(*Water Music*, 1717)等。

67 Pure Joy

I must live almost alone like one who has been banished, I can mix with society only as much as true necessity demands. If I approach near to people a hot terror seizes upon me and I fear being exposed to the danger that my condition might be noticed. Thus it has been during the last six months which I have spent in the country...what a humiliation for me when someone standing next to me heard a flute in the distance and *I heard nothing*, or someone heard a *shepherd singing* and again I heard nothing. Such incidents drove me almost to despair, a little more of that and I would have ended my life — it was only *my art* that held me back. Ah, it seemed to me impossible to leave the world until I had brought forth all that I felt was within me.... Oh Providence — grant me at last but one day of *pure joy* — it is so long since real joy echoed in my heart....

— *Beethoven*

六十七　完美的快樂

我必須像個被放逐的人那樣，過一種近乎獨處的生活。我與社會的接觸僅限於滿足一些完全是最基本的需要。我一旦接近其他人，就有一種強烈的恐懼感。我深恐陷入一種危險，即人們可能發覺我的處境。最近我住在鄉下的半年，就是這種狀態……當我身邊站着的人聽到遠處長笛吹奏的樂聲，我卻什麼也聽不見。或是有人聽到一個牧羊人在唱歌，而我還是什麼也聽不到，這對我是多麼大的羞辱啊。這樣的事情把我逼到了幾乎絕望的境地。要是再遇到一些，我恐怕早就結束自己的生命了——然而，正是我的藝術挽救了我。啊，我好像只有把內心的東西都傾瀉出來之後，才可能離開這個世界。哦，上帝啊——無論如何賜給我哪怕一天的完美的快樂吧——我已經很久沒有感受真正的快樂在我心中回蕩了……。

——〔德〕貝多芬

名人簡介

Ludwig van Beethoven（貝多芬）(1770－1827)，德國作曲家，其創作集西方古典樂派（classicism）之大成，開創了浪漫樂派(romanticism)，對後世西洋音樂的發展有深遠影響，主要作品包括交響曲、奏鳴曲、弦樂四重奏曲等。

68 In Nature's Open

You will ask me whence I take my ideas? That I cannot say with any degree of certainty: they come to me uninvited, directly or indirectly, I could almost grasp them in my hands, out in Nature's open, in the woods, during my promenades, in the silence of the night, at the earliest dawn. They are roused by moods which in the poet's case are transmuted into words, and in mine into tones, that sound, roar and storm until at last they take shape for me as notes.

— *Beethoven*

六十八　靈感的來源

你也許會問，我的靈感來自何處？說起這一點，我可沒有絲毫的把握。它們是不邀自來，直接了當地或是曲折迂回地。在大自然懷抱裏、在林間、在散步時、在夜晚的靜謐中、在黎明剛剛開始的那一刻，我幾乎都能抓住靈感。這些靈感由種種情懷激起。要是發生在詩人身上，那麼就形成詩句；發生在我身上，就變成音調，發出聲響、咆哮、怒吼，最後形成我需要的音符。

——〔德〕貝多芬

名人簡介

Ludwig van Beethoven（貝多芬）(1770－1827)，詳見第 67 篇。

69 We Owed Him a Living

He was one of the most exhausting conversationalists that ever lived. Sometimes he was brilliant; sometimes he was maddeningly tiresome. But whether he was being brilliant or dull, he had one sole topic of conversation: himself. What he thought and what he did.

...

The world did owe him a living. What if he did talk about himself all the time? If he talked about himself for twenty-four hours every day for the span of his life he would not have uttered half the number of words that other men have spoken and written about him since his death.

— J. D. Taylor[1]

1. Joseph Deems Taylor (1885 — 1966)：迪姆斯．泰勒，美國作曲家、音樂評論家。

六十九　幸虧有他

他是個健談的人，談得你精疲力竭，像他這樣世上少有。他時而聰慧過人，時而又討厭得使人受不了。不過不論他是機敏過人也好，還是乏味無聊也好，他的話題只有一個——他本人，他的所思所為。

……

這世上有他，真該感謝他才是。要是他確是總在談論自己，又有何妨呢？要是他這一輩子每天二十四小時都談論自己，那他所說的還不及世人在他去世後談論他的一半多。

——〔美〕泰勒

名人簡介

Wilhelm Richard Wagner（理查德・瓦格納）(1813—1883)，德國作曲家、歌劇家，畢生致力於歌劇(自稱"樂劇")的改革，作品有歌劇《漂泊的荷蘭人》(*The Flying Dutchman*,1841)、《唐懷瑟》(*Tannhäuser*,1845)等。

70 Faithful to Music

His first wife spent twenty years enduring and forgiving his infidelities. His second wife had been the wife of his most devoted friend and admirer, from whom he stole her.

...

What if he was faithless to his friends and to his wives? He had one mistress to whom he was faithful to the day of his death: Music. Not for a single moment did he ever compromise with what he believed, with what he dreamed. There is not a line of his music that could have been conceived by a little mind.

— J. D. Taylor[1]

1. J. D. Taylor：迪姆斯．泰勒，詳見第 69 篇的註釋。

七十　忠貞不渝

他的第一位夫人和他生活了二十年，容忍並寬恕了他的不忠行徑。而他的第二位夫人曾經是他最忠實的朋友和仰慕者的妻子。瓦格納是從這朋友那裏把她偷來的。

……

如果他對朋友們和太太們都不夠忠誠的話，那又何妨呢？他至死都忠於一位情人：音樂。他從未有一刻背棄他所信仰的，他所夢想的。他的音樂作品中，沒有一行是普通人能構思出來的。

——〔美〕泰勒

名人簡介

Wilhelm Richard Wagner（理查德．瓦格納）(1813—1883)，詳見第 69 篇。

71 A Camellia

Somewhere in the wide world there is an actor — and a good one — who never eats celery without thinking of me. It was years ago, when I was playing Camille. In the first scene, you will remember, the unfortunate Armand takes a rose from Camille as a token of love. We had almost reached that point, when, as I glanced down, I saw that the flower was missing from its accustomed place on my breast.

What could I do? On the flower hung the strength of the scene. However, I continued my lines in an abstracted fashion, and began a still hunt for that rose or a substitute. My gaze wandered around the stage. On the dinner table was some celery. Moving slowly toward it, I grasped the celery and twisted the tops into a rose form. Then I began the fateful lines:

"Take this flower. The life of a camellia is short. If held and caressed it will fade in a morning or an evening."

七十一　一朵茶花

在這廣闊世界的一個地方有一位男演員——一位很好的演員——每當他吃芹菜的時候，總會想起我。那是許多年前的事。那次我演茶花女。第一場裏，你們一定記得，不幸的阿爾芒從茶花女手中接過一朵玫瑰花，作為愛情的信物。我們快演到這一處了，這時我低頭一看，發現我胸前習慣有花的地方沒有花了。

我怎麼辦？花是這一場戲的關鍵。不過我繼續心不在焉地說我的台詞，開始不動聲色地尋找那朵玫瑰花或替代物。我的目光在舞台上四處打量。飯桌上有芹菜。我慢慢地走近桌子，抓起芹菜，把頂端部分扭曲成玫瑰花形狀。然後我開始說出至關重要的台詞：

“你把這朵花拿去吧。茶花活的時間很短。拿在手裏，撫摸它，這花過了上午或者過了晚上就會凋謝。”

名人簡介

Clara Morris（莫里斯）(1847—1925)，美國女演員，曾在紐約戴利劇團（美國著名劇作家和劇院經理 Augustin Daly 創辦）演出(1870—73)，又在許多地方巡迴演出，直到90年代。她被公認為感情演員，茶花女是她享有盛名的角色之一。著有《舞台生活》(*Life on the Stage*, 1901)、《明星的一生》(*The Life of a Star*, 1906)等。

Hardly able to control his laughter, Armand spoke his lines which ran: "It is a cold, scentless flower. It is a strange flower." I agreed with him.

— C. Morris

阿爾芒差點沒笑出來，說出他的台詞："這是一朵冰冷的、沒有香味的花。這是一朵奇特的花。"我同意他的說法。

——〔美〕莫里斯

72 I Said That First

You may find this hard to believe, but Igor Stravinsky[1] has actually published in the papers the statement, "Music to be great must be completely cold and unemotional!" And last Sunday, I was having breakfast with Arnold Schoenberg, and I said to him, "Can you imagine that Stravinsky actually made the statement that music to be great must be cold and unemotional?" At this, Schoenberg got furious and said, "I said that first!"

— A. Schnabel[2]

---

1. Igor Stravinsky (1882—1971)：斯特拉文斯基，俄裔美籍作曲家，20 世紀傑出作曲家之一，早期代表作有舞劇《火鳥》(*L'Oiseau de feu*, 1910)等，中期轉向新古典主義，作品有《聖詩交響曲》(*Symphony of Psalms*, 1930)等，後期多採用序列音樂手法，作品有歌劇《浪子的歷程》(*The Rake's Progress*, 1951)等。
2. Artur Schnabel (1882—1951)：施納貝爾，奧地利鋼琴家、教師，以演奏貝多芬作品見長，著有《對音樂的見解》(*Reflections on Music*, 1933)等。

七十二　是我先說

你也許覺得這件事令人難以置信，不過斯特拉文斯基確實在報上發表過以下言論："音樂欲變得偉大，必須是絕對冷漠，絲毫不帶感情色彩的！"上週日，我和勳伯格共進早餐的時候，我對他說："你想得到嗎？斯特拉文斯基真的說過那樣的話。音樂欲變得偉大，必須是絕對冷漠，絲毫不帶感情色彩的！"聽了這話，勳伯格異常憤怒，說："這話是我先說的！"

——〔美〕施納貝爾

名人簡介

Arnold Schoenberg（勳伯格）(1874—1951)，奧地利裔美籍作曲家、音樂理論家，二十世紀傑出作曲家之一，創立十二音體系（12-tone system），作品有交響詩《佩利亞斯與梅麗桑德》(*Pelleas and Melisande*, 1902—03)等。

73 Where Do You Live?

When Clement Attlee[1] was prime minister, I was asked to meet him at Stratford-upon-Avon at a supper at the Falcon Hotel after he had attended a performance (one I was not in myself). I sat next to his daughter and the conversation turned on where we lived.

"I have a very convenient home in Westminster," I remarked. "So easy to walk to the theatre. And where do you live?"

Miss Attlee looked distinctly surprised and replied curtly, "Number ten, Downing Street[2]."

— J. Gielgud

1. Clement Richard Attlee (1883—1967)：艾德禮，英國首相(1945—1951)、工黨領袖。
2. Number ten, Downing Street：唐寧街十號，位於倫敦，為首相官邸所在地，源自該處地產所有人、英國政治家 Sir George Downing (1623—1684)。

七十三　您住哪兒？

艾德禮任首相期間，一次，他看完一場演出後(那次演出我沒參加)，邀請我到艾汶河畔斯特拉特福的獵鷹飯店與他共進晚餐。我坐在首相千金的旁邊。席間，我們的話題轉到了我們的住處。

我說：“我在威斯敏斯特的家很近便，步行去劇院不費事。那您住哪兒呢？”

艾德禮小姐顯得很驚訝，隨即草草地回答說：“唐寧街十號。”

——〔英〕吉爾古德

名人簡介

Sir John Gielgud（吉爾古德）(1904－)，英國演員，以扮演莎士比亞劇中角色聞名，因對戲劇有貢獻被封為爵士。

74 A Jumble Sale

I have always felt that a man often betrays his friendships in his will. So there is a clause in mine in which I name all of the people I have loved or who have been nice to me. And to each of them I leave a little thing — either an object or a little money. I tried to remember them all. When I made my will, my lawyer looked at me in dismay. "Mr. Menotti," he said, "this is not a will. This is a jumble sale!"

— *C. Menotti*

七十四　舊貨拍賣

我總覺得一個人常會在遺囑裏背棄友誼。因此我在遺囑裏有這麼一條：把所有我愛過的人或曾經待我不錯的人的名字逐一列出，而且還給他們每個人都留點東西——或是一件物品，或是一小筆錢。我盡力要記起所有這些人。我立遺囑的時候，我的律師沮喪地看着我說："門諾蒂先生，這不是一份遺囑，倒是一次舊貨拍賣！"

——〔美〕門諾蒂

名人簡介

Gian Carlo Menotti（門諾蒂）(1911—)，意大利裔美國作曲家，主要作品有歌劇《阿米莉亞赴舞會》(*Amelia Goes to the Ball*, 1937)、《領事》(*The Consul*, 1950)等。1958年曾在意大利創辦"兩個世界音樂節"。

Politicians
政治家

75 Follow His Example

I know a gentleman who was such a good manager of his time that he would not even lose the small portion of it which the calls of nature obliged him to pass in the necessary-house; but gradually went through all the Latin poets in those moments. He bought, for example, a common edition of Horace[1], off which he tore gradually a couple of pages, carried them with him to that necessary place, read them first, and then sent them down as a sacrifice to ... : this was so much time fairly gained, and I recommend you to follow his example.

— *Chesterfield*

---

1. Horace：賀拉斯 (公元前 65—8)，古羅馬詩人，部分作品曾對西方的詩歌產生過很大影響。

七十五　學他的樣

我認識一位先生，他是個珍惜時間的能手，連上廁所方便的一點點時間也不浪費。他竟然逐漸利用如廁的時間通讀了全部拉丁詩人的作品。舉個例子說，他買了一冊普通版的賀拉斯詩集，一次次地從書上撕下二、三頁來帶進廁所，先是閱讀，然後當作便紙扔進……。就是這樣，他多得到很多時間。我建議你們也效法他。

——〔英〕切斯特菲爾德

名人簡介

Philip Dormer Stanhope Chesterfield（切斯特菲爾德）(1694—1773)，英國外交家、作家，曾任英國駐荷蘭大使(1728—32, 1744)、國務大臣(1746—48)。他與英國詩人蒲柏 (Pope)、作家斯威夫特 (Swift)、法國哲學家伏爾泰 (Voltaire) 等名人過從甚密。以所著《致兒家書》(*Letters to His Son*, 1774)、《給教子的信》(*Letters to His Godson*) 而聞名。本篇選自他寫給兒子的一封信。

76 An Escape of More Importance

At Newport[1] we took in a number of passengers, among whom were two young women traveling together, and a sensible, matron-like Quaker lady, with her servants. I had shown an obliging disposition to render her some little services, which probably impressed her with sentiments of good will toward me; for when she witnessed the daily growing familiarity between the young women and myself, which they appeared to encourage, she took me aside, and said, "...these are very bad women; I can see it by all their actions; and if thee art not upon thy guard, they will draw thee into some danger; they are strangers to thee, and I advise thee, in a friendly concern for thy welfare, to have no acquaintance with them." As I seemed at first not to think so ill of them as she did, she mentioned some things she had observed and heard that escaped my notice, but now convinced me she was right. I thanked her for her kind advice, and promised to follow it. When we arrived at New York,

1. Newport：紐波特，位於美國羅得島州 (Rhode Island)。

七十六　躲過劫難

在紐波特，我們的船上來了許多乘客。他們當中有兩個結伴旅行的年輕女子。還有一位通情達理，穩重的貴格會女教徒，身邊帶着幾個僕人。我真心實意地想為她做些小事情。這也許使她對我有很好的印象。她目睹我與那兩名女子日漸親密起來，而且她們表現出慫恿的態度，於是她把我拉到一邊説："……這是兩個很壞的女人，根據她們的表現我能看得出來。如果你不加提防，她們會讓你陷於危險的。你並不瞭解她們。出於友誼，也是為了你好，我勸你不要和她們交往下去了。"由於我一開始似乎並沒有像她那樣把她們想得那麼壞，她提到一些我沒注意到而她卻看到聽到的事情。這時，我相信她是對的。對她的忠告我向她表示感謝，答應照她的話去做　。我們到達紐約的時

名人簡介

Benjamin Franklin（富蘭克林）(1706—1790)，美國政治家、哲學家、科學家。他是美國啟蒙運動的開創者、美國獨立革命的領導人之一。他參加了許多重要的活動，如起草獨立宣言(1776)、出使法國(1776—85)、與英國簽訂承認美國獨立的和約(1783)等。他有不少科學研究和發明，其中避雷針為世人皆知。他著述甚多，代表作有《自傳》(*Autobiography*)。本篇軼事即選自該書，描述了作者18歲時出外謀生旅途中險遭不測的經歷。

they told me where they lived, and invited me to come and see them; but I avoided it, and it was well I did; for the next day the captain missed a silver spoon and some other things, that had been taken out of his cabin, and, knowing that these were a couple of strumpets, he got a warrant to search their lodgings, found the stolen goods, and had the thieves punished. So, though we had escaped a sunken rock, which we scraped upon in the passage, I thought this escape of rather more importance to me.

— Benjamin Franklin

候，那兩個女子把她們的住址告訴給我，還邀請我去看她們，可是我沒去。我這樣做做對了。因為第二天，船長發現少了一把銀匙和一些別的東西。這些東西是從他的臥艙裏被偷走的。當他得知那兩名女子是妓女時，便取得搜查令，搜查了她們的住處，找到了被偷的東西，讓這兩個小偷受到了懲罰。這樣，雖然我們避開了航程中擦肩而過的暗礁，而對我來說，我的這次躲過她們才是更為重要的。

——〔美〕富蘭克林

77 No Desire of Profiting

... having, in 1742, invented an open stove for the better warming of rooms, and at the same time saving fuel, as the fresh air admitted was warmed in entering, I made a present of the model to Mr. Robert Grace, one of my early friends, who, having an iron-furnace, found the casting of the plates for these stoves a profitable thing, as they were growing in demand. To promote that demand, I wrote and published a pamphlet, ... This pamphlet had a good effect. Governor Thomas was so pleased with the construction of this stove, as described in it, that he offered to give me a patent for the sole vending of them for a term of years; but I declined it from a principle which has ever weighed with me on such occasions, viz., that, as we enjoy great advantages from the inventions of others, we should be glad of an opportunity to serve others by an invention of ours; and this we should do freely and generously.

An iron-monger in London, however, assuming a good deal of my pamphlet, and working it up into his own, and making some small changes in the machine, which rather

七十七　無意發財

……1742年，我發明了一種敞開式爐子，用於改進室內取暖。同時，這種取暖爐能夠節省燃料，因為新鮮空氣在進入室內時就被加熱了。我把這種爐子的樣品作為禮物送給我的老友羅伯特·格雷斯先生。他有一隻熔鐵爐，發現澆鑄這種爐子的金屬板有利可圖，因為這種金屬板的需求量正在增長。為了促進這種需求，我撰寫並出版了一本小冊子，……這本小冊子的效果頗佳。湯姆斯總督對小冊子中所描繪的爐子的結構極為滿意，表示要給我為期若干年的獨家經營的專利權。但是我婉言拒絕了，這是由於在這種場合有一準則對我是很重要的，即當我們受益於他人的發明創造時，我們應當為有機會利用自己的發明創造為他人服務而感到高興。這種事情我們不應該索取報償，而應該慷慨大方。

然而，倫敦的一個小五金商僭取了我小冊子上的大量內容，歸入了他自己的發明。他只是對爐子作了一些小小

名人簡介

Benjamin Franklin（富蘭克林）(1706－1790)，詳見第 76 篇。

hurt its operation, got a patent for it there, and made, as I was told, a little fortune by it. And this is not the only instance of patents taken out for my inventions by others, though not always with the same success, which I never contested, as having no desire of profiting by patents myself, and hating disputes.

— *Benjamin Franklin*

的改動。這反而使爐子的運作受到損害。他在當地獲得了專利權。有人對我說，他因此還發了小財。別人拿我的發明作為自己的專利，不只是這一例，儘管他們並不一樣順利。我從不為此與他們爭辯，因為我沒有靠專利發財的願望，而我也不喜歡與人爭辯。

——〔美〕富蘭克林

78 The Witness Fled

He had set his great eyes on the man and searched him through and through; then, as the cause went on, and this fellow's perjury was not yet called for, Webster looked round again to see if he was ready for the inquisition. The witness felt for his hat and edged toward the door. A third time Webster looked on him, and the witness could sit no longer. He seized his chance and fled from the court and was nowhere to be found.

— *V. W. Brooks*[1]

---

1. Van Wyck Brooks (1886—1963)：布魯克斯，美國文學史家、評論家和傳記作家，著有《論當代文學》(*On Literature Today*, 1941)等，寫的傳記涉及Mark Twain、H. G. Wells、Emerson、Washington Irving、Whitman 等多位名作家。

七十八　不攻自破

他用一對大眼睛望着那個人，對他仔細打量。隨着案件審理的進展，韋伯斯特乘那傢伙還沒被傳喚得以提供偽證詞的時候，又一次掉轉頭去看那傢伙是不是已經準備好回答法庭的審問。那個證人摸索着他的帽子，側着身子往門口挪動。韋伯斯特第三次朝他投去目光。這時候那個證人再也坐不住了。他抓住時機迅速離開法庭，逃得無影無蹤。

——〔美〕布魯克斯

名人簡介

Daniel Webster（韋伯斯特）(1782—1852)，美國律師和政治活動家，參與過許多重要的國務活動和法律案件處理。曾兩次任美國國務卿(1841—43；1850—52)，也競選過總統。他的才能出眾。本篇描述他做律師時的一次出色表現。

79 Above Her Level

A brilliant but uncouth and almost grotesque lawyer[1] and politician from the backwoods, with no inherited social position or distinction, marries a showy, popular belle, who considers herself an aristocrat in the limited circle which is all she knows, and feels that she is condescending vastly in accepting the husband whose only asset is an extremely nebulous future. Then the husband shows an unexampled capacity for growth and development, intellectual and spiritual, if not social, and the wife, remaining to the end the narrow rural aristocrat she was in the beginning, is decidedly left behind. The strange destiny which made the man who was to save the future of American democracy a typical American and a typical democrat was hardly equal to making him also an ideal husband, at any rate an ideal husband for such a wife. Mrs. Lincoln[2] married Lincoln with condescension and hoped that he might rise to her level, or even above it. He did, and so far as to be altogether beyond

---

1. lawyer：指 Abraham Lincoln (林肯)。
2. Mrs. Lincoln：Mary Todd Lincoln (1818－1882)，於 1842 年與林肯結婚。

七十九　高於期望

一位卓越的，但欠文雅的、近乎怪異的律師和政壇人物來自邊遠地區，沒有世襲的社會地位和榮譽，娶了一個愛炫耀的、討人喜歡的漂亮小姐。在她唯一熟悉的有限的社交圈內她自命高貴，覺得同意嫁給一位以虛幻未卜的前途為僅有財產的丈夫，對她來說是莫大的屈尊俯就。後來這位丈夫就算不是在社交方面，也在心智發展方面表現出絕無僅有的能力。而他的妻子自始至終是個狹隘的鄉村貴族，很明顯趕不上他了。奇怪的命運使這個注定要拯救美國民主之前途的人成為一個典型的美國人和典型的民主主義者，可是不能使他成為一個理想的丈夫，那怕就是這樣一個妻子的理想丈夫。林肯夫人屈尊嫁給了林肯，希望林肯能夠高攀到她的社會地位，甚至高過她的地位。這一點

名人簡介

Abraham Lincoln（林肯）(1809－1865)，美國第十六任總統，當過律師、眾議院議員。任總統期間的南北戰爭中，採取革命性措施，取得戰爭的勝利。戰後遇刺身亡(1865)。

her limited power of ascent. She made a useful helpmate for a practical, aggressive lawyer in Springfield, Illinois. As the wife of the great, dreaming, smiling, creating democratic statesman of the modern world, she was just a trifle over-parted.

— G. Bradford[3]

3. Gamaliel Bradford (1863—1932)：布雷德福，美國傳記作家，善於揭示歷史人物內心活動。主要著作有《美國人李將軍》(*Lee the American*, 1912)、《聯邦人物群像》(*Union Portraits*, 1916)、《婦女群像》(*Portraits of Women*, 1916)等。

他做到了，而且完全超過了她攀登社會階梯的能力。她成為伊利諾斯州斯普林菲爾德的一名講究實際的、敢作敢為的律師的得力伴侶。但是，作為現代社會的這位偉大的、有理想的、微帶笑容的、有創意的民主政治家的妻子，她有點不能勝任。

——〔美〕布雷德福

80 Tragedies of Money

How simple his financial ideas were appears in his reported remark shortly before his election as President: "I have a cottage at Springfield and about eight thousand dollars in money.... I hope I shall be able to increase it to twenty thousand, and that is as much as any man ought to want." As a matter of fact, his estate was much larger than this at the time of his death.

Mrs. Lincoln no doubt did her best. In the early days she made her own dresses and she had always moments of violent economy.... "... I often laugh and tell Mr. Lincoln that I am determined my next husband shall be rich." ... "... If he knew that his wife was involved to the extent that she is, the knowledge would drive him mad. He is so sincere and straightforward himself, that he is shocked by the duplicity of others. He does not know a thing about my debts, and I value his happiness, not to speak of my own, too much to allow him to know anything. This is what troubles me so much. If he is re-elected, I can keep him in ignorance of my

八十　入不敷出

他在理財方面的想法是多麼單純，這一點在他當選總統前不久的講話中被報導出來，他說：“我在斯普林菲爾德有一幢農舍，大約值八千美元。……我希望能把它增值到二萬美元。那是一個誰都該想要的數目。”事實上，在他去世的時候，他房產的價值大大超過這個數目。

林肯夫人無疑已竭盡所能了。在最初的那些日子裏，她自己動手縫製衣服，經濟情況一直是緊張拮据的。……“……我常常笑着對林肯先生說，下一次我一定要嫁給一個有錢的丈夫。”……“……如果他知道他的妻子被拖累到她現在這個樣子，這會使他發瘋的。他這個人非常真誠直率，對別人的表裏不一會感到震驚的。他對我的債務一無所知。我很珍惜他的幸福，更不用說我自己的幸福了，所以不想讓他知道欠債的事。就是這樣使我十分頭痛。如果他連任，我可以讓他仍舊不知道我的事情。但是，如果他

名人簡介

Abraham Lincoln（林肯）(1809—1865)，詳見第 79 篇。

affairs; but if he is defeated, then the bills will be sent in and he will know all." Such are the domestic tragedies of money.

— *G. Bradford*[1]

1. G. Bradford：布雷德福，詳見第 79 篇的註釋。

落選了，那麼，那些帳單就會送來，他就會全知道了。”當家理財竟是這樣使人尷尬難堪。

——〔美〕布雷德福

81 His Powerful Physique

Like every strong man, he once saved his own life. An assassin...had fired one shot at him and was about to fire a second, this time at closer range. It would have been fatal, had not Bismarck seized the man's right hand and hurled the weapon to the ground. On another occasion, when he was younger, he had plunged into the water after a man who was drowning — and for the rest of his life, among all the insignia of honor which "go with the make-up of a minister," he took pride only in the medal commemorating this rescue. Again, he saved Prussia[1], when the king was about to yield to popular pressure and to abdicate, by taking hold of the king's scabbard and literally shaking him into a mood of self-defence.

None of these three equally important acts would have been possible without the assistance of his powerful physique. Wherever he went, he was the biggest man present.... Emperors of the French and of the Russians[2], kings, princes,

---

1. Prussia：普魯士，德意志帝國的主要成員。
2. the French and ... Russians：俾斯麥（Bismarck）曾經是普魯士駐俄國 (1859－62) 和法國(1862) 的使節。

八十一　體魄魁梧

他像所有強壯的人一樣，曾經拯救過自己的性命。一個行刺者……已經朝他開了一槍，正準備開第二槍，這一次的射擊距離更近了。俾斯麥抓住了那人的右手，用力奪過武器扔到地上，要不是這樣的話，那將會是致命的一槍。另有一次，那時他還比較年輕，他為搶救一個溺水者而跳入水中。在他以後的一生裏，在"與宰相服飾相配"的所有榮譽勳章中，只有這塊紀念那次救人的獎章他引以為榮。再有一次，他挽救了普魯士。當國王屈服於民眾的壓力準備退位的時候，他抓住國王的劍鞘，確確實實把國王晃動得下決心自衛。

這三次意義都很重大的行動中，如果不是得力於他那魁梧的體格，無論哪一次都不可能成功。不管他到哪裏，他總是在場人中最強健者。……法國和俄國的皇帝，還有

名人簡介

Otto Eduard Leopold von Bismarck（俾斯麥）(1815—1898)，普魯士政治活動家，德意志帝國於1870年成立後第一任宰相，宣稱德國的問題必須以"血和鐵"解決，故有"鐵血宰相"之稱。

and princesses — all were impressed to see him stoop as he came through the door and then draw himself up again to his full height. Generals and politicians, most of them his opponents for one reason or another, were often astounded, and even terrified, by his build.

— *E. Ludwig*[3]

3. E. Ludwig：路德維格，詳見第 4 篇的註釋。

國王、王子和公主都見過他弓着身子進門然後再挺起高大身軀的樣子，這給他們留下很深的印象。將軍和政客當中的大部分都因某種原因是他的對頭人，但是他的魁梧身材常常令他們驚愕甚至恐懼。

——〔德〕路德維格

82 The Bridal Bed

An embarrassed newlywed employee came to Baldwin and told him he had broken the bridal bed. Baldwin said it could be repaired free at the family ironworks, but the man feared it would make him the laughing stock of all his mates. So the broken bed was brought to the back door of Baldwin's house at night, wheeled through the hall the following morning, and taken across the road for repair as if it were Baldwin's own.

— *L. Howard*[1]

1. Lady Lorna Howard：霍華德夫人，鮑德溫的女兒。

八十二　新婚的牀

一個神情窘迫的新婚僱員來找鮑德溫，説他把新婚的牀弄壞了。鮑德溫説，可以免費在自家的鐵匠舖裏修理。可是這位僱員害怕朋友們會把他當做笑柄，所以把那張弄壞的牀在晚上送到鮑德溫家的後門，第二天早上才裝上車，穿過他家的客廳，送到路對面去修理，好像是鮑德溫自己的牀。

——〔英〕霍華德

名人簡介

Stanley Baldwin（鮑德溫）(1867—1947)，英國保守黨政治家，歷任政府重要職位，曾三次任首相和第一財政大臣(1923—24;1924—29;1935—37)，又曾任商務部大臣(1921—22)、財政大臣(1922—23)、樞密大臣(1931—35)等要職。

83 A Terrorist's Brother

During his boyhood the assassination of Alexander II[1] took place; and as a student of law at Kazan[2] he felt the results of this anarchistic attack, sharing with his comrades such resentment and impatience at their slave-like life under the knout as might be expected of so obstinate and freedom-loving a temperament. His elder brother was his teacher and his ideal. He was the first translator of Marx and Hegel[3], and initiated the younger Lenin in these authors. The brother planned a conspiracy in Saint Petersburg against the new czar six years after the last assassination. But he, with the other conspirators, was arrested in the street on the morning set for the attack, was brought to court, and hanged. This was the last attempt at terrorism.

Lenin was seventeen.... His courage and his love made him rise to the occasion, but being cool and intelligent,...

---

1. Alexander II (1818一1881)：亞歷山大二世，俄國沙皇，因鎮壓革命運動被刺殺。
2. Kazan：喀山，俄羅斯城市。列寧曾在喀山大學學習法律。
3. Marx and Hegel：馬克思(1818—1883)，詳見第 7 篇；黑格爾(1770—1831)，德國古典唯心主義哲學家，其哲學成為馬克思主義哲學的理論來源之一。

八十三　獨闢蹊徑

在他的童年時代發生了亞歷山大二世被刺事件。後來他在喀山大學學習法律時，感受到這種無政府主義襲擊帶來的後果。他和他的同志們具有堅毅不拔、熱愛自由的性格，對在沙皇皮鞭下奴役般的生活多麼憤慨難忍，確屬人們的意料。他的哥哥是他的老師，也是他心中的典範。他第一個翻譯了馬克思和黑格爾的著作，引導他的弟弟列寧讀他們的著作。這位哥哥在那次暗殺事件六年後，在聖彼得堡密謀反對新沙皇。但是他和他的密謀者一起於策動謀反的那天早晨在大街上被捕，送上了法庭，被處絞刑。這是對沙皇恐怖行動進行打擊的最後一次嘗試。

當時列寧十七歲。……勇氣和愛心促使他站出來對此作出反應。但是列寧很冷靜、理智，……他明白，成功不

名人簡介

Vladimir Ilyich Lenin（列寧）(1870—1924)，蘇聯共產黨組建者和蘇維埃國家締造者。

Lenin realized that success could not be obtained at one stroke, but must be carefully prepared for over a period of years, perhaps during a whole lifetime. Thus, by the logic of history, the brother of Russia's last destructive terrorist became Russia's first constructive socialist. Marx was his brother's will and testament; Lenin saw in Marx the intellectual weapon which might succeed where the bomb had failed.

— *E. Ludwig*[4]

---

4. E. Ludwig：路德維格，詳見第 4 篇的註釋。

可能一蹴而就，而必須經過若干年的精心準備，或許要經歷畢生的時間。作為歷史的必然結果，俄國最後一個破壞性的恐怖主義者的弟弟就這樣成了俄國第一個建設性的社會主義者。馬克思是他哥哥的遺願。列寧把馬克思看作思想武器，這種武器在炸彈不能起作用的地方可能會奏效。

——〔德〕路德維格

84 Spoken English

We thought we knew the English language, having even translated a whole book from English into Russian when we were in Siberia. I had learnt English in prison from a teach-yourself book, but had never heard a word of it spoken. Now that we were in London, we found we could not understand a single word, and nobody understood us. At first this was very amusing, and Vladimir Ilyich joked about it. However, he soon got down to learning the language. We started going to all kinds of meetings, always standing in the front row and carefully studying the speaker's mouth. We went very often to Hyde Park where speakers addressed the passing crowds on different subjects. We were particularly keen on listening to one man, who spoke with an Irish accent which we found easier to understand. We learnt a great deal by listening to spoken English.

Afterwards, through an advertisement, Vladimir Ilyich got in touch with two Englishmen who wanted to exchange lessons, and he began studying with them. He got to know the language quite well.

— *Krupskaya*[1]

---

1. Nadezhda Konstantinovna Krupskaya (1869—1939)：克魯普斯卡婭，俄國革命家、教育家，列寧的夫人。

八十四　學說英語

我們以為自己是通曉英語的，因為我們在西伯利亞的時候，甚至把一本英文書全部譯成了俄文。我是在監獄裏從一本自學課本上學得英語的，但是從來沒聽別人說過一句英語。現在我們來到倫敦，卻發現連一句話都聽不懂，而誰也聽不懂我們的話。起初這種情況讓人覺得很有趣，弗拉基米爾·伊里奇也因此開起了玩笑。然而，他很快就開始認真地學起這種語言來。我們開始參加各種會議，總是站在前排，仔細琢磨說話人的嘴形。我們特別常去海德公園，在那兒演講人就不同的話題向過路的人群發表演講。我們尤其喜歡聽一個人的演講，他說話帶愛爾蘭口音，我們覺得更容易聽懂。通過聽別人講英語，我們學到很多。

在這以後，通過一則廣告，弗拉基米爾·伊里奇聯繫上了兩個想要交換課程的英國人。於是，他跟着他們學起來了。結果，他的英語學得相當不錯。

——〔俄〕克魯普斯卡婭

名人簡介

Vladimir Ilyich Lenin（列寧）(1870－1924)，詳見第 83 篇。

85 Love Affair with Painting

My father, Winston Churchill, began his love affair with painting in his 40s, amid disastrous circumstances[1]. ...

...

... in the mid-1920s he won first prize in a prestigious amateur art exhibition held in London. Entries were anonymous, and some of the judges insisted that Winston's picture...was the work of a professional, not an amateur, and should be disqualified. In the end, they agreed to rely on the artist's honesty and were delighted when they learned that the picture had been painted by Churchill.

Historians have called the decade after 1929, when the Conservative government fell and Winston was out of office,

1. disastrous circumstances：指他被免去內政大臣和海軍大臣的職務而下台。

八十五　愛上繪畫

我的父親溫斯頓．邱吉爾在四十多歲的時候愛上繪畫。他那時正處於災難性的困境中。……

……

……20世紀20年代中期他在倫敦舉辦的一次有威望的業餘畫展上獲得頭獎。參賽作品都是匿名的。有些評判人堅持說，邱吉爾的畫……是專業畫家的，不是業餘畫家的，所以應被取消資格。最後，他們同意信賴畫家的誠實。當他們得知這幅畫是邱吉爾畫的，都感到高興。

歷史學家們把1929年以後的十年稱作邱吉爾失勢的年代。在這期間，保守黨政府垮了台，他也就跟着下野。政

名人簡介

Sir Winston Churchill（溫斯頓．邱吉爾）(1874—1965)，英國政治家、著作家、保守黨領袖，歷任政府許多重要職務，最為有名的是擔任英國首相(1940—45;1951—55)，在第二次世界大戰期間領導英國人民對德國法西斯作戰。他著作甚多，如《世界危機》(*The World Crisis*, 1929)、《馬爾博羅生平》(*Marlborough： His Life and Times*, 1938)、《第二次世界大戰》(*The Second World War*, 1954)、《英國民族史》(*History of the English-Speaking Peoples*, 1958)等，獲1953年諾貝爾文學獎。

his wilderness years[2]. Politically he may have been wandering in barren places, a lonely fighter trying to awaken Britain to the menace of Hitler, but artistically that wilderness bore abundant fruit. Of the 500-odd canvases extant, roughly 250 date from 1930 to 1939.

— *M. Soames*[3]

---

2. wilderness years：習語in the wilderness指在政治上失勢，因而這裏指政客或政黨在野、不當政的時候。
3. Mary Soames (1922—)：瑪麗．索姆斯，邱吉爾的女兒。

治上他也許是個徘徊在不毛之地的孤獨戰士，極力地想要喚醒英國認清希特勒的威脅。但是在藝術上，那個荒野卻是碩果纍纍。在現存的五百多幅油畫中，大約有二百五十幅是他 1930 年到 1939 年期間的作品。

——〔英〕索姆斯

86 Hobbled Across

Winston Churchill[1] came to the Augusta[2] at eleven o'clock, which saw the dramatic handshake of Roosevelt and Churchill at the gangway. They prolonged the clasp for the photographers, exchanging smiling words.

... Roosevelt stood a full head taller, but he was pathetically braced on lifeless leg frames[3], clinging to his son's arms, his full trousers drooped and flapping. ...

... Leaning on his son's arm and on a cane, Franklin Roosevelt, in a blue suit and gray hat, lurched out on the gangplank, laboriously hitching one leg forward from the hip, then the other.... With each step, the tall President tottered and swayed. ...

His foot touched the deck of the Prince of Wales[4]. Churchill saluted him and offered his hand. The brass band

---

1. Winston Churchill：邱吉爾，詳見第 85 篇。
2. the Augusta：美國軍艦名。1941年8月羅斯福與邱吉爾秘密會談，簽訂了大西洋條約，從此美國正式向希特勒德國宣戰。羅在此軍艦上迎接了邱吉爾。
3. lifeless leg frames：羅斯福幼時因患小兒麻痺症而下肢癱瘓。
4. the Prince of Wales：邱吉爾所乘的英國軍艦，文中描述羅斯福的回訪。

八十六　海上密談

溫斯頓．邱吉爾於十一點鐘登上了奧古斯塔號軍艦。軍艦上的人都看到羅斯福和邱吉爾在舷梯口戲劇性的握手。他們相互微笑地寒暄，延長握手的時間，讓攝像師們拍照。

……羅斯福站立着，比邱吉爾高出一個頭。但令人感到惋惜的是，他靠沒有生氣的腿骨架支撐着，緊靠着他兒子的胳膊，他的長褲寬鬆地懸垂着，迎風飄動。……

……富蘭克林．羅斯福身着藍色套裝，頭戴灰色禮帽，倚着他兒子的胳膊，拄着拐杖，一瘸一拐地走上跳板，費勁地把一條腿從胯部起整個兒向前邁出去。接着是另一條腿蹣跚向前。…… 這位高個子總統每向前挪動一步，他的身子就要踉蹌地搖晃一次。……

他的腳踏上了"威爾士親王號"的甲板。邱吉爾向他致

名人簡介

Franklin Delano Roosevelt（富蘭克林．羅斯福）(1882—1945)，美國第32任總統，在第二次世界大戰中，他對建立反法西斯同盟作出重大貢獻。

burst forth with "The Star Spangled Banner[5]." Roosevelt stood at attention, his chest heaving, his face stiff with strain. Then, escorted by Churchill, the President hitched and hobbled all the way across the deck, and sat.

— *Herman Wouk*[6]

---

5. "The Star Spangled Banner"：美國國歌。
6. Herman Wouk (1915—)：沃克，美國小說家。第二次世界大戰中，他在海軍服役。本篇選自他寫的小說《戰爭風雲》(*The Winds of War*)。

意，向他伸過手去。銅管樂隊奏響了“星條旗”，羅斯福肅然立正，胸脯起伏着，緊張地繃着臉。之後，總統在邱吉爾陪同下搖搖晃晃地走過甲板，坐了下來。

——〔美〕沃克

87 The Youngest Hosted[1]

Before proceedings, Churchill[2] and Stalin[3] agreed that Roosevelt, the only head of state[4], would preside at the first formal session. Everything was so relaxed it did not seem possible that the conference was about to make decisions involving the fortunes of millions of people. There was nothing of the strain so frequently found on great occasions.

Roosevelt's first words were in a light vein[5]. As the youngest of the three, he said, he welcomed his elders. Churchill was the most eloquent, saying, "In our hands we have the future of mankind." As host, Stalin welcomed his guests and then added: "Now let us get down to business."

— *Charles Bohlen*[6]

---

1. 本篇描述 1943 年德黑蘭會議（Tehran Conference）的情況。
2. Winston Churchill：邱吉爾，詳見第 85 篇。
3. Joseph Stalin (1879—1953)：斯大林，蘇聯共產黨總書記、蘇聯部長會議主席。
4. the only head of state：當時蘇聯和英國的元首分別是最高蘇維埃主席和君主，斯大林和邱吉爾都不是一國元首，只有羅斯福是一國元首。
5. vein：state of mind; mood (情緒)。
6. Charles Eustis Bohlen (1904—1974)：波倫，美國外交家，第二次世界大戰期間多次陪同羅斯福出席重要會議。

八十七　主持會議

會議開始之前，邱吉爾和斯大林一致同意讓唯一的國家元首羅斯福主持第一次正式會議。會議上的一切都是十分輕鬆，似乎會議並不會作出涉及到千百萬人命運的決定，一點都沒有那種在重大場合經常出現的緊張氣氛。

羅斯福輕鬆地作了開場白。他說，作為三人中年紀最輕者，他歡迎他的兄長。邱吉爾的口才最好，他說："我們的手掌握着人類的未來。"斯大林作為東道主，向客人表示了歡迎，接着又說："現在讓我們開始正題吧。"

——〔美〕波倫

名人簡介

Franklin Delano Roosevelt（羅斯福）(1882—1945)，詳見第 86 篇。

88 An Excellent Speaker to Interpret for

I was a little nervous at the prospect of interpreting for the President[1]. The Moscow Conference of Foreign Ministers[2] had been good practice, but this meeting[3] was at the highest level. In the few minutes I had with the President before his first meeting with Stalin[4], I outlined certain considerations regarding interpreting. I asked if he would try to remember to break up his comments into shorter periods of time. I said that if he talked very long, his Russian listeners, not understanding what was said, would probably lose interest. On the other hand, speaking for two or three minutes at a time would hold their attention and make my job infinitely easier. Roosevelt understood, and I must say he was an excellent speaker to interpret for, showing in a variety of ways consideration for my work.

— *Charles Bohlen*[5]

---

1. the President：指 Franklin Delano Roosevelt (羅斯福)。
2. The Moscow Conference of Foreign Ministers：該會議於 1943 年在莫斯科舉行。作者陪同美國國務卿參加了會議。
3. this meeting：指 1943 年德黑蘭會議。
4. Joseph Stalin (1879—1953)：斯大林，詳見第 87 篇的註釋。
5. Charles Bohlen：波倫，詳見第 87 篇的註釋。

八十八　善解人意

想到要為總統當翻譯，我有點緊張。莫斯科外長會議對我是一次很好的練習，但是這一次會議是最高級的。在總統就要與斯大林第一次會晤之前，我有幾分鐘同總統在一起。我概括地說了一些有關翻譯的想法。我問他是否能盡量記住把要說的話分成時間較短的若干段落。我說如果時間講得很長，聽他說話的俄國人會因聽不懂而失去興趣。相反，每次講二三分鐘，會保持他們的注意力，也會大大方便我的翻譯工作。羅斯福明白了我的意思。我應該說，他是一位很便於為他當翻譯的演說家。他從各個方面體諒我的工作。

——〔美〕波倫

名人簡介

Franklin Delano Roosevelt（羅斯福）(1882—1945)，詳見第 86 篇。

89 To Fine Everybody

One bitter cold day they brought a trembling old man before him, charged with stealing a loaf of bread. His family, he said, was starving. "I've got to punish you," declared La Guardia. "The law makes no exception. I can do nothing but sentence you to a fine of ten dollars."

But the Little Flower[1] was reaching into his pocket as he added, "Well, here's the ten dollars to pay your fine. And now I remit the fine." He tossed a ten-dollar bill into his famous sombrero. "Furthermore," he declared, "I'm going to fine everybody in this courtroom fifty cents for living in a town where a man has to steal bread in order to eat. Mr. Bailiff, collect the fines and give them to this defendant!" The hat was passed and an incredulous old man, with a light of heaven in his eyes, left the courtroom with a stake of forty-seven dollars and fifty cents.

— *B. Cerf*[2]

---

1. Little Flower：拉瓜迪亞的綽號。
2. Bennett Alfred Cerf (1898 — 1971)：塞爾夫，美國出版家和編輯，創辦 Random House 出版社。

八十九　誰之過？

一個寒冷的日子，他們把一個哆哆嗦嗦的老頭帶到了他的面前，指控老頭偷了一個麵包。老人說他的家人都在挨餓。“我得懲罰你，”拉瓜迪亞宣佈說，“法律是容不得例外的，我只得判你罰款十美金。”

但是拉瓜迪亞把手伸進自己的口袋，接着說：“嗯，這十塊錢為你付罰金，現在你的罰款我就給免了。”他把十元紙幣扔進了他的那頂很出名的闊邊帽。他宣佈說：“還有，我要對本法庭的每一個人罰五十美分，因為你們生活在這樣的一個鎮上，有人為吃飯還不得不去偷麵包。庭警先生，你來收這些罰款，然後把這些錢都給這個被告！”那頂帽子在大家手裏傳送。那個不敢相信眼前情景的老頭閃爍着興奮的眼神，拿着共有四十七元五角的一筆錢走出了法庭。

——〔美〕塞爾夫

名人簡介

Fiorello Henry La Guardia（拉瓜迪亞）(1882—1947)，美國政治家，曾任紐約市長，以力反貪污著稱。後任聯合國善後救濟總署署長。

90 Never a Man Minister

When my daughter, Julie Eisenhower, interviewed Mrs. Meir for her book, *Special People*, she asked how it had felt to be appointed the first woman foreign minister in 1956. [Mrs. Meir's] reply was characteristic. "I don't know," she said with a smile. "I was never a man minister."

— *R. Nixon*[1]

1. Richard Milhous Nixon (1913—1993)：尼克松，美國第37任總統。

九十　女外長

我的女兒朱莉·艾森豪威爾為她的那本題為《特殊人物》的書採訪梅厄夫人的時候，問她1956年被任命為第一位女外長時感覺怎樣。〔梅厄夫人〕回答得很有特色。她笑着說："我不知道，因為我從來沒當過男部長。"

——〔美〕尼克松

名人簡介

Golda Meir(梅厄夫人)(1898—1978)，以色列女政治活動家，以色列總理(1969—74)，生於烏克蘭基輔，1906年移居美國，1921年移居巴勒斯坦，從事猶太復國事業，曾任以色列外交部長(1956—66)、以色列工人黨總書記(1966—68)，幫助組建勞動黨(1967)。原名Goldie Mabovitch，1917年結婚後姓名用Goldie Meyerson，1956年起改用現在的希伯來姓名。

Others
其他

91 She Was Justified

In May, 1855, after six months of labour, Miss Nightingale[1] could look with something like satisfaction at the condition of the Scutari[2] hospitals. ... One simple comparison of figures was enough to reveal the extraordinary change: the rate of mortality among the cases treated had fallen from 42 per cent to 22 per thousand. But still the indefatigable lady was not satisfied. The main problem had been solved — the physical needs of the men had been provided for; their mental and spiritual needs remained. She set up and furnished reading-rooms and recreation-rooms. She started classes and lectures. Officers were amazed to see her treating their men as if they were human beings, and assured her that she would only end by "spoiling the brutes." But that was not Miss Nightingale's opinion, and she was justified. The private soldier began to drink less, and even — though that seemed impossible — to save his pay. Miss Nightingale became a banker for the army, receiving and

---

1. Miss Nightingale：指南丁格爾。
2. Scutari：斯庫台，阿爾巴尼亞城市。

九十一　善待傷員

1855年5月，經過半年的艱苦工作之後，南丁格爾小姐對司庫台醫院的狀況可以說滿意了。……一個簡單的數字比較足以說明那種非同尋常的變化：經過治療的傷員的死亡率從百分之四十二下降到千分之二十二。但是這位不屈不撓的女士仍舊不滿足於現狀。主要的問題已得到了解決，即士兵的物質需求已經得到滿足，但是精神和宗教方面的需要還是有待解決的問題。她把閱覽室和娛樂室建立起來，並配備了設施。她開設了各種課程和講座。軍官們驚異地看到她把士兵當作人來對待。他們要她確信，她最終會“寵壞那些粗野的人”的。但是南丁格爾小姐不這樣想。結果她是對的。那個普通士兵不再那麼酗酒了，而且——儘管看似一件不可能的事情——他把錢省了下來。南丁格爾小姐成了軍隊的銀行代理人。每個月她都要接收大

名人簡介

Florence Nightingale（南丁格爾）(1820—1910)，英國女護士，近代護理學和護士教育創始人，以在克里米亞戰爭(1854—1856)中改善傷員護理工作而聞名。

sending home large sums of money every month. ... during the next six months, £71,000 was sent home.

— *L. Strachey*[3]

3. Lytton Strachey： 斯特雷奇，詳見第 29 篇的註釋。此篇選自 "Florence Nightingale"一文。該文被認為是*Eminent Victorians*中的最佳篇。

筆錢，然後又把錢寄回國去。……在以後的六個月中她寄了七萬一千英磅。

—〔英〕斯特雷奇

92 Very Near to Death

Amid all these activities, Miss Nightingale took up the further task of inspecting the hospitals in the Crimea itself. The labour was extreme, and the conditions of life were almost intolerable. She spent whole days in the saddle, or was driven over those bleak and rocky heights in a baggage cart. Sometimes she stood for hours in the heavily falling snow, and would only reach her hut at dead of night after walking for miles through perilous ravines. Her powers of resistance seemed incredible, but at last they were exhausted. She was attacked by fever, and for a moment came very near to death. Yet she worked on; if she could not move, she could at least write; and write she did until her mind had left her; and after it had left her, in what seemed the delirious trance of death itself, she still wrote. When, after many weeks, she was strong enough to travel, she was to return to England, but she utterly refused. She would not go back, she said, before the last of the soldiers had left Scutari[1].

— L. Strachey[2]

---

1. Scutari：斯庫台，阿爾巴尼亞城市。
2. L. Strachey：斯特雷奇，詳見第 29 篇的註釋。

九十二　差點沒死

在所有這些活動中，南丁格爾小姐對克里米亞本區的醫院作了進一步的視察工作。工作十分艱苦，生活條件幾乎令人難以忍受。她連續幾天人不離馬鞍，或是乘着行李車翻越那些荒涼貧瘠、布滿巖石的高地。她有時候站在鵝毛大雪中好幾個小時，常常在深更半夜步行幾英里，穿越危機四伏的深谷之後，才回到她的帳棚裏。她的抵抗力好得令人難以置信，但是最終還是消耗殆盡。她發起高燒，曾一度病得差點沒死。然而她卻繼續工作。如果無法走動,她至少還能寫。她就這樣一直寫，直到神志不清。出現這種情況之後，她在這看似昏死狀的迷睡中還是在寫。幾個星期以後，她康復到可以走路了，這時，她可以返回英國了，但她堅決不走。她說，她要在最後一名傷員撤離司庫台之後才回國。

——〔英〕斯特雷奇

名人簡介

Florence Nightingale（南丁格爾）(1820—1910)，詳見第 91 篇。

93 Something Sensational

He undertook the work precisely as Gordon Bennett[1] had commissioned him: "No matter how much it costs, find Livingstone[2]! We Americans don't know what it means to be beaten.... If he is dead, we'll produce his bones. But in any case we'll find Livingstone. We'll give them something sensational!"

... The greatest newspaperman of America was sending his greatest reporter.

And he went, in fact, with American speed, and found what he had set out to find. "My mission to find Livingstone was very simple, and was a clear and definite aim. All I had to do was to free my mind from all else, and relieve it of every earthly desire but the finding of the man whom I was sent to seek. To think of self, friends, banking-account, life-insurance, or any worldly interest but the one sole purpose

---

1. James Gordon Bennett, Junior (1841—1918)：小貝內特，美國新聞工作者，《紐約先驅報》(*New York Herald*)創始人 J. G. Bennett 之子，除繼任該報編輯外，又創辦《紐約電訊晚報》(*New York Evening Telegram*, 1867)。
2. David Livingstone (1813—1873)：利文斯通，英國傳教士、探險家，深入非洲從事傳教和地理考察活動達30年。

九十三　聳人聽聞

他進行這項工作嚴格遵照戈登．貝內特委任他的要求："不惜代價，要找到利文斯通！我們美國人不知道什麼叫失敗。……如果他死了，我們也要找到他的屍骨。但是，不管什麼情況我們都要找到利文斯通。我們要為人們提供有轟動效應的新聞！"

……美國最了不起的新聞界人物派出了他最了不起的新聞記者。

實際上，他是以美國式的高速度去那裏的，找到了此行要尋找的目標。"我尋找利文斯通這個使命是非常簡單的，是一個明白無疑的目標。我要做的一切就是集中精力，使自己的思想擺脱掉一切塵世的欲念，而只是去找我受命尋找的那個人。如果只考慮自己、朋友、銀行戶口、人壽保險，或者任何物質利益， 而不去想此行唯一的目的

名人簡介

Henry Morton Stanley（斯坦利）(1841—1904)，英國記者、探險家，以在中非洲救出失蹤的探險家Livingstone和多次到非洲探險並全面勘探剛果地理（1874－77）而聞名。本文作者把他視為美國人。

of reaching the spot where Livingstone might happen to rest, could only tend to weaken resolution. Intense application to my task assisted me to forget all that I had left behind, and all that might lie ahead in the future."

— *E. Ludwig*[3]

3. E. Ludwig：路德維格，詳見第 4 篇的註釋。

——到達利文斯通可能停留的地方——那就會削弱我的決心。專心致志地執行我的任務，有助於忘掉已經拋在腦後的一切，也不去想將來可能發生的一切。”

——〔德〕路德維格

94 All This Is Unparalleled

The discovery of the Congo...shows this American[1] at the height of his energy. It was this trip which has been compared to the voyage of Columbus — and as an exploit it has been considered even greater. What plagues, mutinies, and perils this man survived during his nine hundred and ninety-nine days in the Congo, what he endured in his thirty-two battles with the natives — all this is unparalleled, and gives us evidence that any obstacle can be surmounted. For once in his life, Stanley was caught in the high winds of heroism. Following a river across a continent, to the point where it empties into the sea! Into the sea! This time Stanley did not find a human[2]; as the greatest of his achievements, he found the sea[3].

— *E. Ludwig*[4]

---

1. this American：指 Henry Morton Stanley (斯坦利)。
2. a human：指 David Livingstone，詳見第 93 篇的註釋。
3. the sea：指 the Atlantic (大西洋)。
4. E. Ludwig：路德維格，詳見第 4 篇的註釋。

九十四　無與倫比

發現剛果……表明這位美國人正處於他精力的最旺盛時期。被比喻成哥倫布航海的正是他的這次遠航。作為一項偉績，人們甚至認為這次航海更加偉大。在剛果的九百九十九天裏，他從瘟疫、兵變和各種危險之中幸免於難，他在與土著的三十二次戰鬥中經受了多麼大的磨難——這一切都是史無前例的。這一切向我們表明，任何障礙都是可以克服的。在斯坦利的一生中就這一次，他在英雄氣概的鼓舞下，一鼓作氣，沿着一條橫貫大陸的河流一直來到它入海的地方！入海的地方！這一次，斯坦利不是找到一個人，他找到的是大海，這是他最大的成就。

——〔德〕路德維格

名人簡介

Henry Morton Stanley（斯坦利）(1841—1904)，詳見第 93 篇。

95 My Last Name

I was born a slave on a plantation in the state of Virginia. ...

...

When the war[1] finally ended and the day of freedom came, it was a glorious moment to all on our plantation. ...

...

When I appeared at the school for the first time, I found myself with a major difficulty — I had no last name. As long as I could remember, I had been simply called "Booker." Before going to school I had never imagined that it was necessary to have another name. When I heard the school roll called, I noticed that all the children had at least two names, and some of them had what seemed to me the luxury of having three! This was a real problem because I knew that the teacher would ask me for at least two names and I had only one. When the time came for registering my name, however, an idea occurred to me which I thought would make

1. the war：指美國南北戰爭(the Civil War, 1861－65)，戰爭後宣佈奴隸解放。

九十五　我該姓什麼？

我出生時就是弗吉尼亞州一個種植園的奴隸。……

……

戰爭終於結束，自由的一天來到了，這對我們整個種植園的人是個輝煌的日子。……

……

我第一次上學的時候，發現我有個很大的難題——我沒有姓。就我記憶所及，大家一直叫我"布克"。上學前我從來沒想過我該有個姓。當我聽到學校在點名的時候，我看到所有孩子的姓名至少有兩個部分，有些孩子的姓名有三個部分，我好像覺得這是個奢侈！這確是個難題，因為我知道，老師至少要我說出兩個部分，而我只有一個。可是輪到該登記我姓名的時候，我有了個想法，我認為這個想法解決了目前情況的需要。這樣，當老師問我的全名

名人簡介

Booker Taliaferro Washington（布克．華盛頓）(1856—1915)，美國著名教育家，黑奴出身，因他對教育事業有不朽貢獻，經國家決定，在他家鄉樹立了國家紀念碑。本篇選自他寫的自傳《出身奴隸》(*Up from Slavery*, 1901)。

me equal to the situation. So when the teacher asked me what my whole name was, I simply told him "Booker Washington", as if I had been called by that name all my life; and by that name I have since been known.

— B. Washington

時，我痛快地告訴他我叫“布克·華盛頓”，就好像我生來就叫這個姓名似的。從此我就用這個姓名了。

——〔美〕布克·華盛頓

96 Offering Biscuits to a Criminal

I once remarked to Shaw[1] that Webb seemed to me somewhat deficient in kindly feeling. "No," Shaw replied, "you are quite mistaken. Webb and I were once in a tram car in Holland eating biscuits out of a bag. A handcuffed criminal was brought into the tram by policemen. All the other passengers shrank away in horror, but Webb went up to the prisoner and offered him biscuits." I remember this story whenever I find myself becoming unduly critical of either Webb or Shaw.

— *B. Russell*[2]

---

1. George Bernard Shaw (1856 — 1950)： 蕭伯納，英國劇作家、評論家，費邊社(Fabian Society)創建人之一，獲 1925 年諾貝爾文學獎，主要劇作有《凱撒和克婁巴特拉》 (*Caesar and Cleopatra*, 1900)、《人與超人》 (*Man and Superman*, 1903)、《巴巴拉少校》 (*Major Barbara*, 1905)等。
2. Bertrand Russell (1872 — 1970)： 羅素，英國哲學家、數學家、邏輯學家，獲1950年諾貝爾文學獎，主要著作有《數學原理》(*Principia Mathematica*, 1910 — 13)、《數理哲學導論》 (*Introduction to Mathematical Philosophy*, 1919)等。

九十六　囚犯與餅乾

有一次，我對蕭伯納說，我覺得韋布這人有點缺乏友善。蕭伯納回答說："不是的，你可大錯特錯了。有一次，在荷蘭我和韋布乘電車，吃着裝在包裹的餅乾。後來，一名上了手拷的囚犯被幾名警察押上了車。別的乘客出於恐懼，全都縮到了一邊。而韋布卻走上前去，給了那犯人一些餅乾。"每當我發覺自己對韋布或是蕭伯納挑剔時，我便會想起這樁事情。

——〔英〕*羅素*

名人簡介

Sidney Webb（韋布）(1859—1947)，英國經濟學家、社會史學家，費邊社（Fabian Society）創建人之一，倡導費邊社會主義，參與重組倫敦大學及制定教育方案工作，著有《英國的社會主義》(*Socialism in England*, 1890)、《工聯主義史》(*History of Trade Unionism*, 1894)等。

97 He Suffered More from the Drink Habit

Poor man[1], he prided himself on having the most brilliant editorial staff in the United States, but he paid high for the privilege: every one of them was a periodical or steady drinker, and there was a memorable occasion when all of them were down at Los Gatos[2] taking — or pretending to take — the Keeley cure[3], and he had to get out the paper himself with the aid of the printers. He used to say that no one suffered more from the drink habit than he, although he never drank, himself.

— *G. F. Atherton*[4]

---

1. Poor man： 指 William Randolph Hearst (赫斯特)。
2. Los Gatos：屬加利福尼亞州的一個小城市，位於舊金山以南，離 Hearst 的家不遠。
3. the Keeley cure：Leslie E. Keeley (1832 — 1900)，凱利，美國醫生，他研究出一種治療酒精中毒的方法。他的診所設在 Los Gatos。
4. Gertrude Franklin Atherton (1857 — 1948)：艾瑟頓，美國女小說家，共寫小說六十多部，主要作品有《征服者》(*The Conqueror*, 1902)、《黑公牛》(*Black Oxen*, 1923) 等。

九十七　不酗酒更受罪

真可憐，他以擁有全美國最精良的編輯人員而自豪。不過他為這一優越條件付出很高的代價。這些僱員都愛喝酒，有的時不時喝，有的一貫喝。有一件事令人難忘。一次，所有人員都去洛斯加托斯進行——或假裝進行——凱利法治療，他不得不在一些印刷工的幫助下親自出版報紙。他總説，儘管自己滴酒不沾，可是他吃足酗酒惡習的苦頭，誰也比不過他。

——〔美〕艾瑟頓

名人簡介

William Randolph Hearst（赫斯特）(1863－1951)，美國報業巨頭，創建赫斯特報系，曾擁有25種日報、11種週刊和多種雜誌。

98 A Croesus[1]

Not that he resorted to display and prodigality. His house and his manner of living were both quiet and distinguished, and in the best taste. He was a Croesus without passions and without collections. He never spent money lavishly; occasionally he bought a beautiful picture, or a rare tapestry, or expensive books. Nor did he ever succumb, like a miser, to the intoxication of mounting sums. To artists and deserving young people, he gave financial assistance from his own funds. But although he proclaimed his doctrines in totally anti-capitalistic terms, and had formulated sound measures against inheritance and other causes of accumulated wealth, he spent his life in the atmosphere of corporations and banks, thinking in the language of stocks and dividends, and never abandoning this field for any other.

— *E. Ludwig*[2]

---

1. Croesus：富翁，源自公元前六世紀小亞細亞一個國家的極為富有的國王名。
2. E. Ludwig：路德維格，詳見第 4 篇的註釋。

九十八　富翁

他不是為了要炫耀和揮霍。他的住宅和生活方式既安靜又顯赫，品味很高雅。他是個大富翁，但是並不追求物欲，也不是收藏家。他花錢從不揮霍，偶爾買幅漂亮的畫，或者稀有的掛毯，或者一些貴重的書。他從不像個守財奴那樣陶醉於不斷增長的錢財。對於藝術家和年輕有為者，他用自己的存款給予資助。他的言論是完全反對資本主義的，也制定了有效措施以防止繼承及聚積財富的其他根源。儘管是這樣說，他的一生仍舊是在公司和銀行的環境中度過的，日常想的是股份和紅利，從未放棄這個行業而從事其他行業。

——〔德〕路德維格

名人簡介

Walther Rathenau（拉特瑙）(1867—1922)，德國企業家、德國民主黨創建人之一，曾任(德意志聯邦共和國)通用電氣公司(AEG)總裁、外交部長等職，被民族主義極端分子暗殺。

99 The Roof Leaks

In 1937, Wright built a house in Wisconsin for industrialist Hibbard Johnson and his family. One rainy evening Johnson was entertaining some distinguished guests for dinner when the roof began to leak. The water seeped through the ceiling directly above Johnson himself, dripping steadily onto the top of his bald head. Irate, he put a call through to Wright in Phoenix, Arizona. "Frank," he said, "you built this beautiful house for me and we enjoy it very much. But I have told you the roof leaks, and right now I am with some friends and distinguished guests and it is leaking right on top of my head." Wright's reply was heard by all. "Well, Hib," he said, "why don't you move your chair?"

— S. C. Johnson[1]

1. Samuel C. Johnson：約翰遜，屬美國約翰遜實業家家族，該家族因生產蠟製品而著名。

九十九　屋頂漏雨

1937年賴特為實業家希伯爾德·約翰遜全家在威斯康星州建造了一座住宅。一個下雨的夜晚，約翰遜正在宴請一些貴客，這時屋頂開始漏雨。雨水從約翰遜上面的天花板滲漏，不停地滴落在他光禿的腦袋上。他很生氣，打了個電話給住在亞利桑那州鳳凰城的賴特，他說："弗蘭克，你為我造了這幢漂亮的房子。我們很喜歡它。不過我對你說過屋頂漏雨。現在我正招待一些朋友和貴客。雨水恰好漏到我的頭上。"賴特的回話大家都聽得見，他說："嗯，希伯，你挪一下椅子不行嗎？"

——〔美〕約翰遜

名人簡介

Frank Lloyd Wright（賴特）(1867—1959)，美國建築師，曾擔任美國名建築師、芝加哥學派代表人物沙利文(Louis Sullivan, 1856—1924)的助手。賴特是草原式建築風格(Prairie School)的主要代表。他設計的建築甚多，很有特色，如紐約拉金大廈(Larkin Building, 1904)、紐約古根海姆博物館(Guggenheim Museum, 1943—59)、東京帝國飯店(Imperial Hotel, 1915—22)等。他的著述有《自傳》(*Autobiography*, 1932)、《有機建築》(*An Organic Architecture*, 1939)、《美國建築》(*American Architecture*, 1939)等。

100 Standing Erect on a Parapet

As the sun came up ...he might have been seen by his fellow officers (and he certainly was seen by the Germans) standing erect, adventurous, and oblivious on a parapet. One hand held his field glasses to his eyes, the other was clenched in excitement as the infantry just ahead charged through a wood. His adjutant — call him Smith, for the purpose of this story — stood at his elbow. Machine-gun bullets were hissing and hitting all around. A captain jumped up out of the trench and touched the general on the arm. "If I might suggest, sir," he said, "your position is dangerous. The machine guns are reaching here."

"Eh, eh, what's that? Oh, yes, quite right, quite right. Thank you, Smith" — this with a glare at his adjutant — "get down in that trench at once."

— *Woollcott*[1]

---

1. Alexander Humphreys Woollcott (1887 — 1943)：沃爾考特，美國記者和作家，著有《呼喊與低語》(*Shouts and Murmurs*, 1923)、《羅馬燃燒的時候》(*While Rome Burns*, 1934)等。

一百　身先士卒

太陽剛升起……他就可能被軍官同事們看到(他肯定也讓德國軍看見了)，直着身子，冒着危險，不顧一切地站在掩護土垛上。他一手拿着雙筒望遠鏡觀望，另一隻手興奮地攥成拳頭。這時，前面的步兵部隊衝過了樹林。他的副官——為了方便敘述暫且叫他史密斯——就站在他的身旁。這時候機關槍的子彈嗖嗖地四處亂飛。一名上尉從戰壕裏跳出來碰了碰將軍的胳膊。他說："長官，我覺得您站的位置太危險了。機槍已經打到這裏了。"

"嗯，嗯，怎麼了?哦，是啊，說得對，說得對。謝謝你，史密斯。"——他一邊瞪視副官，一邊說——"馬上下戰壕去。"

——〔美〕沃爾考特

名人簡介

Douglas Macarthur(麥克阿瑟)(1880—1964)，美國將軍，第二次世界大戰期間任西南太平洋盟軍總司令。本篇記述他在第一次世界大戰中率領陸軍時的軼事。

外國名人軼事一百則 = 100 anecdotes of eminent people / 王堅,華蘇揚編譯. --臺灣初版. --臺北市：臺灣商務, 2000[民89]
面； 公分. --(一百叢書：32)
中英對照
ISBN 957-05-1646-1(平裝)

1. 世界 - 傳記 - 幽默, 軼事, 諷刺等

781 89002867

一百叢書㉜

外國名人軼事一百則

100 Anecdotes of Eminent People

定價新臺幣 280 元

編譯者 王 堅/華蘇揚
責任編輯 金 堅
出版者
印刷所 臺灣商務印書館股份有限公司
臺北市重慶南路 1 段 37 號
電話：(02) 23116118 · 23115538
傳眞：(02) 23710274
讀者服務專線：080056196
E-mail：cptw @ ms12.hinet.net
郵政劃撥：0000165-1 號
出版事業登記證：局版北市業字第 993 號

• 1999 年 7 月香港初版
• 2000 年 4 月臺灣初版第一次印刷
本書經商務印書館(香港)有限公司授權出版

ISBN 957-05-1646-1(平裝) b 26285000